HOW to WRITE PSYCHOLOGY

Laboratory reports and essays

3rd Edition

HOW TO WRITE PSYCHOLOGY

LABORATORY REPORTS AND ESSAYS

3rd Edition

Bruce Findlay

Pearson Education Australia
Unit 4, Level 2
14 Aquatic Drive
Frenchs Forest NSW 2086

www.pearsoned.com.au

Acquisitions Editor: Nicole Meehan
Project Editor: Jane Roy
Editorial Coordinator: Jill Gillies
Copy Editor: Loretta Barnard, Sonnet Editorial
Index compiled by Tricia Waters
Cover design by Ingo Voss
Cover images from Getty Images
Typeset by Midland Typesetters, Maryborough, Vic.

Printed in Malaysia

2 3 4 5 07 06 05 04 03

National Library of Australia
Cataloguing-in-Publication Data

Findlay, Bruce M. (Bruce Malcolm), 1946– .
How to write psychology laboratory reports and essays.

3rd ed.
Bibliography.
Includes index.
For tertiary students
ISBN 1 74009 408 5

1. Psychology – Authorship. 2. Report writing. I. Title.

808.06615

Prentice Hall
An imprint of Pearson Education Australia

Preface

The Australian Psychological Society welcomes the opportunity to continue its association with the publication of this, the third edition of Bruce Findlay's *How to Write Psychology Laboratory Reports and Essays*.

This book is designed as an introductory text for all psychology students engaged in the task of writing undergraduate reports and essays. Pitched at a level somewhere between a typical academic handout on the subject (i.e. distributed by the lecturer to the class just before the lecture) and the comprehensive *Publication Manual* of the APA (used for conventional publication output), it is readable, uses simple language but most importantly, guides the student through this important process.

This style of manual provides an important guide for the structuring of reports, reporting of statistics and citing of references – all mainstream tasks in the discipline of psychology.

As a new edition it offers the following updates and improvements on the previous manual. First, new examples have been introduced to assist students in preparing their own work. Second, extended coverage of electronic and Internet sources have been referenced and the inclusion of a new 'companion website' allows students to practise modules of essay and lab report writing in a self-initiated format. Third, the content has been modified to conform with the 5th edition of the APA Manual and tables and figures have had a facelift in layout to aid the reader in interpretation. As with the previous edition, the third edition introduces students to research ethics and their importance in any practical work or empirical investigation.

As the Manager for Science and Education at the APS, I am pleased to recommend this manual to students and teachers alike, as it reflects the high standards of training and education required by the APS. These standards stipulate that laboratory work, experimentation and essay writing form essential components of an undergraduate program concerned with the study of psychology.

This is an invaluable resource and the content has been prepared by an Australian psychologist whose membership of the Australian Psychological Society reflects his commitment to high professional, academic and ethical standards.

Students are invited to discover more about the functions of the APS and the benefits membership delivers at www.aps.psychsociety.com.au. By joining the APS, students will gain insights into the diversity of the profession of psychology, access to resources and countless opportunities to meet and network with future peers.

Dr Mary Katsikitis, PhD, MAPS
Manager, Science and Education
The Australian Psychological Society Ltd

Introduction

Introduction to students

If you've picked this up to see what it's like – buy it! It'll save you a lot of hassles in your undergraduate psychology career.

Most psychology students do not go on to become the sort of psychologists who publish journal articles. Most psychology departments treat you as if you will! The laboratory reports you will write as an undergraduate are different from those an academic would write, although they are designed to lead you towards that level. This book will give you all the information you need about how to prepare and write psychology laboratory reports and essays in psychology at the undergraduate level, without overburdening you with all those extra touches that are needed for publication.

There is a glossary of those words that are on the tip of your tongue, but whose meaning just escapes you at the moment. There is a list of 1000 commonly misspelled words, to save you dragging out your dictionary. There is an index that will lead you to the help you need for any particular feature of a lab report or essay that is bothering you. There are flow charts of the processes involved in writing a lab report and an essay. There is an example of a lab report that you can use as a sort of graphical index. *If you want some global advice for undergraduate writing in psychology, it is – learn to plan ahead!* It will save you a lot of anxiety of the sort that occurs when your computer fails at midnight and the assignment is due at 9 a.m. the next morning. This book will show you how to learn this valuable skill.

Good writing! It's not nearly as difficult as you might think.

Introduction to staff members

Purpose of the book This small book is intended to address the need for a set of guidelines for writing undergraduate-level psychology laboratory reports and essays. *It is aimed at first- and second-year students*. It is *not* a guide to writing for publication. It does, however, observe the conventions required by the 5th edition of the *Publication Manual* of the American Psychological Association (APA) and it includes the rationale for those conventions, as well as the steps to be taken in producing and presenting psychological research reports and essays. A student who grasps these concepts and learns the conventions will have a sound basis for presenting research in a professional manner, and writing well argued essays, so that the later step of writing for publication should be an easier one to take.

Why such a book is desirable Increasing student numbers and proportionally dwindling resources in Australian universities often result in students spending less time in classes that teach how to write laboratory reports, and in getting less feedback on what they have written. This is particularly true at first-year level. In the past, most psychology departments produced handouts on writing lab reports and essays, but they were often quite brief. They were also frequently produced by staff members who had been writing for publication for some time, and who took for granted a good deal of information that first-year students, in particular, do not know. It has been my experience that many students find the conventions of psychological report writing especially difficult, since the requirements differ both from those of their other tertiary subjects, and from their own previous experience. When students ask questions of staff members, they are often given ad hoc answers, which lead to complaints from students about lack of consistency between staff members about what is expected in lab reports.

Students will find this book useful because it is considerably more detailed than the typical departmental handout, but not as overwhelming as books advising on writing for publication, such as the *Publication Manual* of the APA. Some of the more advanced books are mentioned towards the end of chapters 4 and 5.

Difference from the previous edition The major differences from the previous edition were made to comply with the latest (5th) edition of the APA *Publication Manual*. Although some staff members weren't happy with the suggestion in my previous edition that the format of the Reference list be the old 'hanging indent' I now feel justified, since the latest *Publication Manual* reverted to that convention, and it is certainly easier to read.

The other major change is the use of italics rather than underlining for references, statistics letters, and table titles. Students were frequently irritated by our insistence on underlining, when they had an italics capability on their computers. In spite of my continuing assertions that they need to demonstrate that they can jump through the hoops of convention that a particular discipline sets, they were frustrated that their lab reports didn't look like many of the articles that they read.

I have also expanded the examples of how to reference internet material, since the APA has finally settled on what it expects in the way of those conventions. My prejudice as a lecturer and setter of lab report assignments is still for students to rely on journal articles as their major source, whether they be print or electronic. There is an enormous amount of material accessible on the web, and students, particularly first-year ones, do not have the experience or the critical faculty to evaluate which is the wheat and which the chaff. I'm inclined to be slightly more generous when it comes to essays, but not much!

You can save yourself some teaching time by recommending that students buy and frequently refer to this book. If you are using this book as an aid to your teaching, and have any constructive criticisms to offer, especially about the newer sections, I would appreciate hearing from you.

Bruce Findlay
Lecturer in Psychology
Swinburne University of Technology
PO Box 218, Hawthorn, Vic 3122
email: bfindlay@swin.edu.au

How to use this book

This book has a number of design features which I hope will make it easier to understand the information I want you to know. There are often good and poor examples cited. They will be in tables, because one of the conventions I want you to learn is that illustrative material belongs in tables. The format of the tables throughout this book is the format that you are expected to learn, but in addition, there will be icons to remind you which are good and which are poor examples. They will look like this:

Good examples for you to follow will have this 'tick' beside them.

Poor examples, or formats that I want you to avoid using in your work, will have this 'cross' beside them.

Notes, which will often accompany tables, will have this little 'notepad' icon beside them. Please read them carefully!

Finally, this icon will accompany comments or instructions that require even closer attention than usual. It will refer to things that are absolutely essential for you to be aware of.

Please be aware that the examples throughout the book, illustrating the conventions you need to know about, are not exhaustive. I would not like you to get the idea that these examples are the only way to express those particular conventions, but they are certainly acceptable ways. As you become more comfortable with writing in this style, you will be able to be more creative within the existing conventions.

At the start of Chapters 3 and 5 there are flow charts which indicate the sequence of activities for the successful writing of lab reports and essays, respectively. Those of you who are more visual in your learning styles may find them a useful summary of the process. There are also checklists for lab reports and essays, at the ends of Chapters 4 and 5 respectively, which will help you to plan, and mark off your achievements in your first few assignments. Feel free to photocopy them and use them to measure your progress.

There is also an example of a lab report starting on page 105. This is best used as a quick guide to any particular part of a lab report you need to check on. It is like an index, but doesn't need you to know the exact word or phrase to look up. It is also useful to show you what a finished report looks like.

At the beginning of each chapter there will be a list of keywords. Before reading that chapter, look up these words in the Glossary at the back of the book. This will ensure that when you first encounter them in the context of the chapter they will already be a little familiar. Their meaning should become even clearer as you read through the chapter.

Acknowledgments

Thanks to the many academics who adopted earlier versions of this book for their introductory psychology classes. I am also very grateful to the many students who have expressed appreciation for the earlier editions of this book, and whose comments and experiences have led me to clarify or expand some points. They more than offset the feeling I get that although students are persuaded to buy the book, many seem not to pay attention to it. One first-year convenor set as a lab report the topic I use as an example in the back of the book. The distribution of students' marks, and the errors they made, suggested that a large number of students didn't realise this!

It may not be apparent to the casual reader, but the publications I refer to as examples in Reference lists, and from which I draw good examples of opening sentences, or hypotheses, are most frequently the work of Australasian psychologists. I am impressed by the number of publications produced by my academic colleagues, and the ease with which I can find good examples without looking beyond our shores. I like to think that I am reinforcing the inspiration that they are to their students. I would particularly like to thank Gordana Bruce for her assistance in reminding me of the many ways that students find to lose marks in lab reports. Her experience and skill in gently but firmly guiding students in the desired conventions of psychological writing is greatly appreciated by students and colleagues alike. As ever, the responsibility for any remaining errors must be mine.

Chapter 1

Reasons for writing laboratory reports

IN THIS CHAPTER

1.1 Why write them?

IN ANY SCIENTIFIC DISCIPLINE the body of established knowledge is rarely shaken up by people of the stature of Einstein or Freud. It is more usually added to, drop by drop, by well-reported studies, each on some relatively specific area. When taken together, these all add to what we know – in the case of psychology – about how people think and behave. Hopefully, some of you will go on to contribute to this increase in knowledge. To do so, you will need to know the conventions of reporting your studies.

You may have begun psychology with an interest in the aspects of the discipline that will allow you to learn how to help other people, and so may not anticipate that you will publish research articles in your professional life. However, even if you don't publish studies, you will almost certainly have to read many published reports. Knowing the conventions and being able to critically evaluate other people's work is very important, because you will need to decide whether the material you read is useful and can be applied to your own area of work. To understand how authors reached their conclusions, and to decide how sound or applicable those conclusions are, requires a familiarity with the conventions of psychological reporting.

The majority of students who study an introductory psychology subject, or even complete a three-year degree with a major in psychology, do not go on to become psychologists. To become a psychologist you will need postgraduate training, that is, at least a fourth year, and probably a Master's degree. Most students with an undergraduate degree in psychology find themselves working in management, human resources or human services departments, market research, journalism, the travel industry, or similar areas. A degree with a major in psychology is well considered in the commercial and industrial world, partly because of the experience of quantitative analysis that goes with writing laboratory reports, but mainly because psychology graduates have had very good training in the disciplined and concise reporting of the work they do.

There are therefore three good reasons why you need to learn to write good laboratory reports:

1 The pragmatic reason is that you are expected to do so as part of an undergraduate degree in psychology, and will be assessed on your ability to do so. It is something you need to know to complete your course successfully.
2 A better reason is that as a potential psychologist you need to appraise what other people have written and to report your own research in order to communicate to the community of scientists/practitioners and academics what you have learned from your study of human, or perhaps animal, behaviour.
3 The third reason is that, even if you do not intend to become a psychologist, any occupation will have its own conventions for preparing and writing

> reports of the work you do. Learning the conventions of psychology laboratory reports demonstrates your ability to 'play the game' at a sophisticated level to potential employers. In addition, the generic skills of synthesising material requiring high levels of theoretical and conceptual understanding, as well as reporting your conclusions concisely and on time, are skills that will stand you in good stead in any professional career.

Many undergraduate psychology students are also asked to write essays. In contrast to a laboratory report, which expects you to describe a piece of empirical research, essays usually expect you to make a sustained case for a point of view in some area of psychological interest. Essay writing is also a valued skill, since it also gives you an opportunity to demonstrate the generic skills of assembling and summarising relevant information, critically evaluating it, and coming to a considered conclusion about it in a succinct way.

1.2 What *is* a laboratory report?

A laboratory report (lab report, for short) is a summary of: (a) why you undertook this particular research; (b) what you expected to find; (c) how you actually did it; (d) what you *did* find; (e) how you interpreted the results; and (f) the theoretical and practical implications of the conclusions you drew from those results.

Like most disciplines, psychology has conventions for the reporting of research findings. The amount of material published is so great that readers need to know where in a report to look to find the information they need. From there they can decide whether they want to read the report in more detail. A more or less standard format of psychological reporting is therefore useful.

The reason that psychology has a 'more or less' standard format is that if you look through some of the major psychology periodicals in your library (and I encourage you to do so in the very near future), such as the *Australian Journal of Psychology*, *Journal of Personality and Social Psychology* or *Child Development*, you will find many articles in a format somewhat different to what is usually taught in first- or second-year psychology. The main reason for this difference is that, at the practical level of reporting ongoing research, there are many more complex designs than you usually encounter in your first couple of undergraduate years. Another reason is that a journal article expects a greater familiarity with existing research in the area than that expected of an undergraduate report. However, by your third year you should be approaching a professional understanding of prior research, and your understanding of the conventions of presentation should conform to journal article standard.

The qualitative difference between journal articles and undergraduate lab reports is that the lab report is primarily an exercise in communication, and only secondarily, if at all, a contribution to research. It is important that the messages your reader receives are the ones you, the writer, want to send. Sometimes the fixed format is at odds with this. Nevertheless, it is important that as an undergraduate you become expert at producing the standard format, and once you are completely in control of it, then you can decide whether it is appropriate to 'bend the rules' in particular cases.

The basic rules are that a lab report consists of the following sections in the sequence indicated:

- Abstract
- Introduction
- Method
- Results
- Discussion
- References
- Appendices.

The Abstract is an overview or precis of the report. The rest of the report may be considered as being like an hourglass in shape (Kidder & Judd, 1986). Your Introduction should begin broadly, indicating the area of thought or behaviour under study and why it is being studied, then begin to narrow down as you describe the work of previous researchers whose results have led to your own study. At the end of the Introduction you should state the aims of your study and the specific hypotheses, which are predictions of what results you expected from your study. The Method and Results sections are the most specific, since they state precisely what was done and what results were obtained. The Discussion starts with an interpretation of the results, and the implications of your own study, then becomes broader again, ending with a general conclusion. The References allow others to check the accuracy of your assertions, and the Appendices contain additional material that doesn't need to be included in the body of the report.

1.3 Writing essays at university

An essay in psychology is no different in basic structure from the essays that you will encounter in other tertiary humanities subjects such as literature or sociology. Unlike lab reports, they are not usually divided into sections. They follow the standard essay pattern of having an introduction, a body or discussion, which is the bulk of the essay, and a conclusion. Psychology essays also need a Title page, Abstract, and Reference list. However, essays at tertiary level are somewhat different from those many of you will have experienced at school. The basic difference is that at university you will be expected to be more evaluative of the material you use in your essays. Psychology essays typically ask you to discuss some research, or to compare and contrast particular theoretical perspectives on some area of behaviour, or even specifically to critically evaluate some area of research.

In Chapter 5 I describe what is expected of each of these sorts of instructions, but in essence they expect you to read people's work with a critical eye. What is expected of you as a student with a major in psychology is that you demand particular standards of evidence for the assertions that researchers make before you give any weight to those assertions. This requires critical thinking on your part, and I describe some ways in which you can apply critical thinking to psychological articles in Chapter 2.

The following chapters will deal with: (a) information on critical evaluation of earlier research, conventions of presentation, and the process of producing an assignment, which are common to both lab reports and essays (Chapter 2); (b) what you do to get started when assigned to write a lab report (Chapter 3); (c) detailed instructions on what sort of material goes in which sections of a lab report, and the conventions for presenting it (Chapter 4); advice about essay writing for psychology (Chapter 5); and using the Internet as a resource (Chapter 6).

CHAPTER 2

Writing laboratory reports and essays – common elements

KEYWORDS
argument, assumptions, collaboration, copying, evidence, generic, hypothesis, methodology, operationalisation, participant, placebo, plagiarism, reference, replication, study, theory

IN THIS CHAPTER

THE ASSIGNMENTS THAT GET the best marks are those that not only follow the conventional format, but are also written clearly and concisely. I would also like to emphasise that assignments that get the best marks also meet the requirements of the instructions given, including word limits, and are submitted on time.

This chapter addresses: (a) the thorny problem of the distinction between collaboration and copying; (b) critical thinking and how it can be applied to previous research; (c) writing style, including the appropriateness of personal pronouns; (d) the use of the correct tense; (e) inclusive language; (f) in-text referencing and the need to acknowledge sources of material, thereby avoiding plagiarism; (g) proofreading; and finally, (f) the physical presentation of the report.

2.1 The collaboration/copying distinction

I would like to encourage collaborative study I believe that it is good practice for your professional life, and it will make your university life more enjoyable and fruitful. However, the subject of collaboration in the production of assessable assignments is very controversial. You should always check what the expectations of your lecturer or tutor are regarding collaboration in the preparation of assessable work.

I think it is desirable for first- and second-year undergraduate students faced with writing an assessable lab report to collaborate in study groups to decide on hypotheses, to discuss which references logically lead to them and do or do not support the hypotheses. I think that it is acceptable to decide, in groups, which statistical tests to use. In reports requiring many statistical calculations, even if computer calculated, it *may* be acceptable to share the calculations. However, this view is *not* universal among academics, and again you should always check with your tutor or lecturer about what is acceptable and what is not acceptable at your institution.

The above preparations for writing a lab report, when shared, ensure that you are not misunderstanding the assignment requirements. Collaborating on the preparations for a lab report also allows a sharing of ideas and opinions that hopefully will give you a taste of the intellectual excitement to be experienced in academic research and which makes much of the grind worthwhile.

If your assignment is an essay, the possibilities for collaboration are much more limited. Most lecturers would probably be happy for you to share resources, such as getting hold of references. However, the essay as a literary form is a structured argument for *your* point of view and your marker will expect that such an argument is *your* argument. If you want advice about whether you are on the right track with your essay plan, it is wisest to have a consultation with the lecturer who set the essay topic.

When it comes to writing, your marker needs to be confident that what is written is your own expression, except where explicitly acknowledged. Do not treat this lightly, as plagiarism will be seriously dealt with. At the very least, plagiarism in an assignment will mean a loss of marks, perhaps zero, for that report. At worst, it can and has led to expulsion from Australian universities. Please read carefully the handbook of your institution and any course guides produced by individual departments for subjects you are studying. Such guides usually contain statements about the seriousness with which plagiarism is considered. Ignorance of their contents is not an acceptable excuse if you are caught submitting material identical to that submitted by another student, or containing large slabs of unacknowledged material from books or journal articles. I elaborate on plagiarism from books and journals later in this chapter (section 2.6).

Check with your lecturer or tutor to find out what they consider acceptable in the way of collaboration. My belief is that collaboration should be encouraged at the planning stage of a lab report, or for practical things like sharing references for an essay. However, when it comes to writing the report or essay, it is essential that it is your own work. For this reason, although I will repeatedly stress the need to get assignments proofread, your proofreader should not be a fellow psychology student. You should be writing for an intelligent layperson, and such a person is ideal as a proofreader.

2.2 Critical thinking

In the first chapter I said that tertiary essays in most subjects, but especially in psychology, require you to apply the skill of critical thinking to the books and articles you read in the course of assignments. Critical thinking is not nitpicking or disagreeing with what you read, but showing that you understand the strengths and weaknesses as well as the main ideas of the work in question. For the purposes of preparing a lab report or essay in psychology, a definition of critical thinking is 'a logical and rational process of avoiding one's preconceptions by gathering evidence, contemplating and evaluating alternatives, and coming to a conclusion' (Smith, 1995, p. 2). This is essentially the generic skill of demonstrating your awareness of the strength of a position with regard to the evidence presented in support of it. The application of this skill maintains one of the major values of good science – an organised scepticism and a critical awareness of the need to support any claims you make with adequate evidence.

The scientific method You will probably have been told in some of your early lectures that psychology is a science because of the *way* it investigates thought and behaviour. The scientific method generally starts from a theory, which is a model or belief about the way the world works, operationalises the theory in a particular situation to arrive at a hypothesis or prediction about what will happen in that situation, then tests the hypothesis. Even when the evidence you find supports your hypothesis, you can only gain support for your theory; it can never be proved. In this context, critical thinking is essentially a way of looking at the conclusions that psychologists have drawn on the basis of the theories they have developed, and the hypotheses they have tested, and asking whether those conclusions are warranted by the evidence put forward in support of them.

Deciding whether a researcher's conclusions are reasonable requires several things. You need to try to figure out their assumptions; you need to decide if their hypothesis is a good operationalisation from the theory they begin with; you need to determine if their sample is representative of the population they then draw the conclusion about, and of sufficient size to support what they say; and whether the evidence, statistical or otherwise, actually does support the claim they are making. You also need to decide whether or not there might be another explanation that fits the facts they observed.

It is common in psychological research to compare groups and look for differences. This assumes that there are differences to be found. It is good critical thinking to point out that a researcher appears to assume that there are such differences, commonly sex differences in the area of interest, or differences in ability between any other groups that are being compared. Identifying apparent assumptions shows that you are not taking the researcher's procedure, methodology, or results for granted, but have thought about why he or she made those assumptions, or adopted the approach that they did.

Good critical thinking also means looking at both sides of a position (or perhaps more, since there are often many possible explanations for any particular set of observations). Remember that an experimental report is itself an argument, since it comes to a particular conclusion on the basis of a particular body of data. Even if you want to argue a particular case, it is good to be able to point out arguments against it, if only to say why they don't apply, or are not reasonable. Being able to anticipate and respond to possible objections to your case actually strengthens your position.

Types of weak arguments You should learn to recognise weak arguments in what you read, and avoid them yourself. There are many good books on critical thinking which describe such arguments in detail. One such book is Moore (1995) who points out several types of weak argument. One is the *illegitimate appeal to authority*. A famous person saying something is not evidence of its truth. You would need to describe the evidence itself, rather than rely on the authority of the person making the assertion. *The straw man argument* is where someone misrepresents an adversary's argument, or states an extreme version of it in order to make that argument easier to refute. Another weak argument is *appeal to popular belief*. 'As everyone knows, males are more aggressive than females' is such an appeal. This may well be a commonly held stereotype, but depends heavily on what counts as aggression. You would need to be much more specific and cite evidence rather than make a general assumption that everyone else agrees with you. *Ad hominem* arguments attack the person rather than his or her argument. It may be tempting to consider someone a racist if they argue that different races have different levels of intelligence. However, you should restrain yourself from attacking the character of that person, and confine yourself to the problems with their argument, perhaps that intelligence tests use language forms that are more familiar to dominant groups in a society.

Critically evaluating psychology journal articles One reason that critical evaluation of journal articles is not more formally taught is that there are few clear guidelines for how to go about it. One person brave enough to put his thoughts into print is Sternberg (1993). (You know he's brave because he has also published on subjects like intelligence, love and wisdom!) He argues that there are (at least) eight standards for evaluating the contribution to knowledge of psychology papers, such as integrating into a new, simpler framework, data that had previously required a more complex framework. Sternberg's standards are aimed at practising researchers who are deciding whether something is useful enough to publish, and so they are broader than what is expected of student lab reports; however if you are planning a research career, they are worth examining.

When critically evaluating a psychological article, especially a report of an empirical investigation, you need to ask some general questions of the article as a whole, and some specific questions about particular parts of it. The general questions are ones asking what the paper *does*. Does it:

- replicate previous findings, and/or support existing theories?
- challenge previous assumptions?
- address important social issues?
- distinguish between theories which predict similar outcomes, or resolve an issue where previous theories make different predictions?
- correct flaws in previous research or introduce better methodology?
- address a previously unidentified or unexplored issue?
- present a promising new theory?

You then need to consider *how* it does these things. You can do this by recognising whether the paper:

- presents a novel/insightful/critical/extensive review of relevant literature
- presents the pros and cons of its major argument
- is clear and unambiguous in its arguments
- adequately covers the relevant literature (this might be a big ask for undergraduates, but you should be reading more widely in your higher years).

Having a satisfactory answer to some of these general questions is not the end of the story. You should then ask some more specific questions about the paper. For example:

- Does the paper present clear hypotheses, and have these been well justified?
- Are the hypotheses well operationalised? That is, will testing them produce an adequate answer to the questions the authors are asking?

The adequacy of the operationalisation of the hypotheses has implications for the Method. For example, you could ask questions about the sample, like:

- Is the sample appropriate?
- If it is a fairly special class of people (e.g., university students) do the questions asked apply universally? If the study addresses physiological measures, or sensory perception, it may not matter that an 'unrepresentative sample' has been used. If the question addressed is pretty specific ('how do university students perceive the quality of the teaching they get?') then a university sample *is* appropriate (depending on the representativeness of the university!). Alternatively, if the sample is (as it usually is) North American, can the results be generalised to 'people' or are there cultural implications? If so, are the authors aware of this?

Other methodological questions might include:

- What measures are used? Are they standard scales, or have the authors created their own? Have they reported the psychometric properties (reliability, validity)?
- Is there a control group? Is one appropriate? Have possible order effects been addressed?
- Are the procedures clear enough that you could replicate the study?

When you consider the Results section of the article you are evaluating, don't feel too bad if the statistics are a bit overwhelming! You are not usually expected to comment on the adequacy of the statistics, unless they are of the kind you have already encountered. You should, however, be able to comment on the clarity with which the results are reported. Similarly, are tables or figures interpretable? Does the text make clear what is to be expected from the tables or figures?

Finally, when thinking about the Discussion section of the article, you could ask yourself questions like these:

- How convincing are the results in testing the hypotheses? Are the results clear and unambiguous? Or are they confusing, with no clear pattern? Do the authors admit that results are inconclusive, or, if the results turn out to be more complex than the hypotheses would have led you to expect, do the authors make this clear?
- How well do the authors link their results with previous findings? Are similarities acknowledged and differences explained?
- The implications of the results are very important. Do the authors suggest that the topic or theory should be thought about differently? Do they want to reframe a theory in the light of their results? Are you convinced that their explanation of psychological processes is an improvement over previous research? Do they make clear suggestions for clarifying unclear results, or addressing other questions, which the study may have raised, but were not its original focus?

- Are there any questions in your mind about the adequacy of the methodology in the light of the results? Do the authors admit methodological flaws or make suggestions for how different methodologies might confirm or refute their findings? Do they even address the effectiveness of the methodology?
- How well does the paper address the broader significance of the results (i.e., usefulness or significance to the 'real world')?
- How well does the paper indicate whether particular issues need resolving? Does it suggest how this might be done? Does it identify other factors that may need to be examined to extend our understanding of the processes in question?

In writing a lab report or essay, you will not have space to answer all these questions. The purpose of this sort of interrogation of an article is to help you to decide which articles are most relevant to the hypotheses you may have been given, or to help you develop hypotheses that are realistically supported by sound evidence from previous researchers. Since a good theory is one which is supported in repeated experiments which are operationalisations in different situations, any one study, whether the hypotheses are supported or not, cannot either refute or confirm the theory. All the more reason for you to be able to succinctly suggest just how much that study contributes to justifying the hypotheses you make in your study.

Some problems with journal articles are easier to identify than others – sample types and sizes are simple ones. However, even if a sample is small and unrepresentative, it doesn't mean that the conclusion is implausible (only that the conclusion drawn does not necessarily follow that piece of evidence). You should therefore be cautious about criticising small or student-only samples. You can get around this by saying things like 'Jones's (1993) conclusions, based on a small, college-student sample, were that . . .' Or, alternatively, of course, 'Green's (1995) conclusions, based as they were on a large, community sample from a major city, are more convincing than those mentioned by Black (1993) and Brown (1991).' In contrast, just because a conclusion *can* logically be drawn from a particular result, it doesn't mean that it is the correct one. If you were imaginative enough, you might think of an alternative explanation for the same observed facts. Beware of sounding too dogmatic!

In summary, you should always read research with your critical thinking faculty 'switched on'. You need to be continuously alert to the assumptions behind the researchers' claims; to the strength of the evidence presented in support of those claims; and to the conclusions drawn from the data reported. In short, good science presupposes genuinely critical thinking.

2.3 Writing style

A lab report is a professional presentation of your research. It should not be conversational, chatty or colloquial. Although the report is an argument in support of your conclusions about your results, there is very little room for personal opinion or speculation, and then usually only in the Discussion. The reader is not interested in your unsupported beliefs. The reader wants to know what the results were, and how they influenced what you think. *Always justify a belief statement.*

You have a little more freedom with an essay, especially with regard to personal opinions. However, those opinions must be supported with evidence, and presented in ways that are not dogmatic, and again you must avoid a conversational style. Remember that you are aiming at a professional presentation to your intellectual peers.

While few scientists these days would argue that science is completely objective, your writing should be as objective as you can make it. Objectivity is helped if you keep your sentences short, avoid personal pronouns as much as possible, and give evidence for any assertions you make.

Personal pronouns The use of personal pronouns is currently a matter of some controversy. In the past, it has been very important in report writing to use impersonal constructions, for example, 'The present author favours the argument that . . .' or 'The present investigators concluded that . . .'; or the passive voice, for example, 'Participants were randomly assigned to groups . . .'. In more recent publications you will occasionally find examples such as 'In the next analyses we attempted to replicate previous findings on . . .', or 'To assess whether the . . . manipulations resulted in significant differences in perception . . . we first examined . . .'.

The advantage of the more passive voice is that it helps you to write more objectively. The disadvantage is that it often sounds clumsy. The problem with working in changing times is that you don't necessarily know how your tutor or lecturer will react. You should always ask your tutor or lecturer what they consider acceptable. It is part of the discipline of the subject to learn what is expected and to work within those constraints.

Even when personal pronouns are acceptable, use them in lab reports only when they improve the simplicity or precision of your writing. It is not generally useful to make statements of opinion or speculation beginning 'I believe that . . .', or 'I lean toward the conclusion that . . .'. Such expressions of opinion should be rare, and then usually only in the Discussion. They do not often add to what can be inferred. For example, the statement 'The evidence suggests that social facilitation is purely an arousal effect' is clearly a statement of the author's opinion. Nothing is added by prefacing it with 'In my opinion' or 'I believe that'.

Essays give you more scope for personal opinions, and therefore for the use of personal pronouns. They are usually expected. However, use them sparingly, and justify your expressions of opinion.

Use of different fonts Another problem of working in changing times is how much you should take advantage of changing technology. Many academics, used to writing for publication, will argue that you should not use different font forms (like **bold** or *italics*) for emphasis in your lab report or essay. If in doubt, don't use them. There is a good case for arguing that you should be able to make the required emphasis by the appropriate use of language. My writing style in this book is also more conversational than you should use in a lab report or essay. That's a polite way of saying 'don't do as I *do*, do as I *say*.'

2.4 Using the correct tense

An element of writing style that often confuses students is the tense used. The rule of thumb is that lab reports should be written in the past tense. You are reporting something that has already happened. However, there are exceptions. The exceptions occur when you refer in your report to something that is happening at the time the reader is reading your report. For example, in the Method section you might say, 'The questionnaire used is included as Appendix A.' Present tense is used because it is true as the reader is reading. Similarly, in your Results section you might say, 'These results are summarised in Table 2', since it is also true as the report is being read. Finally, in your Discussion, having reported (in the past tense) whether or not your hypotheses were supported, you could say, 'These results suggest that . . .'. In this case, present tense is used because, although the results were supported (or not), they have implications for the present and future. In the same vein, you could say at the very end, 'In summary, this study indicates that people judge corporations more harshly than individuals', because it is a statement, in the present, of what the study suggests. If in doubt, however, write in the past tense. This is especially true for hypotheses. They should state what you predicted would happen. Look at Table 3 in Chapter 3 for examples of aims and hypotheses.

Essays are typically written in the present tense, except where you are reporting something that has already happened. This is because you are trying, in the present, to convince the reader of your point of view. For example, you might say that 'Smith (1985) performed a study . . .' when describing what Smith did in the past, but you would then say 'Smith (1985) argues that . . .' because Smith's conclusion is still alive and well in the service of your argument, either as evidence for what you want to assert, or as evidence that you have considered points of view other than your own.

2.5 Inclusive language

It is important, in the interests of accuracy and equity, to use gender-neutral language. The major problem with gender-biased language lies in the use of masculine nouns and pronouns when the context includes both genders. Much research, especially Martyna (1978), suggests that readers of both genders think of male persons even when the context suggests that both genders are included.

The best solution is to use plural pronouns. Instead of writing 'The individual who displays prejudice in his personal relations is . . .', write 'Individuals who display prejudice in their personal relations are . . .' Avoid using s/he since it is impossible to pronounce, and he/she, which disturbs the flow of the writing. Further examples of gender-neutral writing are presented in Table 1. On the other hand, avoid carrying this sensitivity to extremes. If all your subjects are male, of course you should use 'he' and 'him' when referring to individuals among them.

Table 1

Examples of Gender-exclusive and Gender-inclusive Language

Original: 'If a subject has a strong tendency to give socially desirable responses in self-description, is it unreasonable to believe that he may also reveal this tendency in his behavior in a learning situation where he is aware of what would be considered socially desirable, namely to learn fast, to do his best?' (Edwards, 1957, p. 89)

Revised: If subjects have a strong tendency to give socially desirable responses in self-description, is it unreasonable to believe that they may also reveal this tendency in their behaviour in a learning situation where they are aware of what would be considered socially desirable, namely to learn fast, to do their best?

Original: 'With sufficient analytical subtlety we can tease out the connections from the behavior of the man in his actual life situation – without the false situation of controlling and manipulating.' (Cattell, 1965, p. 20)

Revised: With sufficient analytical subtlety we can tease out the connections from the behaviour of people in their actual life situations – without the false situations of controlling and manipulating.

Original: 'The goal of the individual includes his expectations for the future, his wishes, and his daydreams. Where the individual places his goals will be determined fundamentally by two factors, namely, by the individual's relations to certain values and by his sense of realism in regard to the probability of reaching the goal.' (Lewin, 1948, p. 113)

Revised: The goals of individuals include their expectations for the future, their wishes, and their daydreams. Where individuals place their goals will be determined by two factors, namely, by the individuals' relations to certain values and by their sense of realism in regard to the probability of reaching the goals.

For the use of gender-neutral language other than pronouns, a thesaurus should help keep you out of trouble. Don't use the collective nouns 'man' or 'mankind', use 'people' or 'humanity'. Don't write 'man an observation station', say 'staff' it. Children need 'nurturing', not 'mothering'.

The issue of sexist language is not trivial. It is vital in the interests of equity. It is also an important part of good communication. Unless you intend your message to refer to one gender only, you need to choose your words carefully so that it is quite clear that you are speaking of people in general. Ask your proofreader to watch out for language that is gender-exclusive, when the exclusion is not justified.

2.6 In-text referencing (or how to avoid plagiarism)

In-text referencing is fairly uncomplicated once grasped, and is identical for both essays and lab reports. However, since it is ruled by strict conventions, it must be adhered to or you will find your work penalised.

Why it is important to avoid plagiarism It is very important that you acknowledge other people's ideas and opinions. Many students think that tutors and lecturers exaggerate the problems of plagiarism. Lecturers and tutors tend to think that students take the problem too lightly. The reason that academics treat plagiarism so severely is that the published word represents the product of their professional labour. If this intellectual effort is used by someone else as if it were that person's own, it is equivalent to theft and is treated as such. Your marker will assume that if you don't acknowledge another source, you intend the reader to believe that the ideas or opinions are your own. If they aren't, you'll be penalised, so be careful.

What is plagiarism? There is no doubt that plagiarism has occurred if you quote a slab of someone's published work and do not acknowledge it as such. However, plagiarism has also occurred if you express someone else's ideas and do not acknowledge that they came from that source. Even when you paraphrase an opinion or description, in your own words and style, you must say where the original idea or description came from.

How do you acknowledge another's work? Acknowledgment of other people's ideas comes in two forms, direct and indirect. *Direct acknowledgment* is when you are saying that some author or authors argue a particular point of view. In your essay or the body of your report, primarily the Introduction and Discussion, give only the surname of the author or authors and the date of publication. Examples are: 'Badcock (1991) stated that . . .' or 'According to McLennan and Bates (1992) . . .' *Do not* use initials, *do not* write the name of the article, *do not* include the page number, and *never* use footnotes, op. cit., loc. cit., or other referencing methods in psychology essays or lab reports.

If there are two authors, always give *both* names every time you refer to them, for example, 'Harre and Secord (1976) found . . .'. If there are three or more authors, you must use all their names the *first* time they are cited, for example, 'McGarty, Turner, Hogg, Davidson and Wetherell (1990) reported that . . .'. If you refer to them again, you can then abbreviate the reference to 'McGarty et al. (1990)'. Once you have referred to an article by name and year of publication, there is no need to repeat the year of publication if you refer to the same author(s) later in the same paragraph. However, when referring again to that article in a *new* paragraph or later in your report, you must again use not only the name(s) but also the date of publication.

Indirect acknowledgment comes when you are explaining, again in your own words, some situation that you did not think of yourself. For example, 'the tendency for people to overestimate personal dispositions and underestimate the effect of the situation as causes of other people's behaviour is called the fundamental attribution error (Vaughan & Hogg, 1998)'. Here you are making a definite statement, and it is not a direct quote, but your own paraphrase, but the names in brackets at the end of the statement or paragraph indicate to the reader that the idea is someone else's. If not all the ideas in the paragraph came from someone else, the onus is on you, the writer, to make clear which ideas are those of other people. Keep a sense of proportion. The lab report is primarily an exercise in communication. Continual interruption of the flow of expression with bracketed references detracts from that communication. This must be balanced against the necessity to acknowledge your sources. The best compromise when integrating material from several sources is to express the ideas in your own words with the sources in brackets at the end of the paragraph. The references should be in alphabetical order of the name of the first author, with the works of any one author in chronological order. For example: (Critchley, 1999; Galligan, 1996, 1998; Reddy & Knowles, 1997). Note that when the authors are mentioned in brackets, their names are joined by an ampersand (&), whereas when using their names in the flow of a sentence they are joined by 'and'. This difference is an example of one of the conventions that you need to learn to demonstrate that you can 'play the game'. When such an acknowledgment is made at the end of a sentence, it should be in brackets, should *not* include any page numbers, and should end with the full stop outside the brackets, as in the example at the start of this paragraph. Table 2 gives some examples of in-text referencing.

Secondary sources It is sometimes necessary to refer to a secondary source; that is, someone that one of your references has referred to but whose publication you cannot get hold of yourself. In such a case, you can say 'Stoner (1961, as cited in Hogg & Abrams, 1987) found that . . .' or 'According to Carlson and Buskist (1999), Piaget's early work indicated . . .'. In such cases only the work that you have actually read is listed in your References. In the above examples, Hogg and Abrams (1987) and Carlson and Buskist (1999) should be listed in your Reference list, but *not* the authors they refer to. Secondary sources of any sort are generally frowned upon when you reach the higher undergraduate years, because you should be personally checking to make sure that you

Table 2

Examples of In-text Citation of References

One author:
Buzwell (1996) suggested that . . .
. . . was found (Buzwell, 1996).

Two authors:
Bates and McLennan (1994) indicated that . . .
. . . was found (Bates & McLennan, 1994).

Three to five authors:
Use all authors' names the first time, but thereafter use the name of the first author and 'et al.' followed by the date. Note the comma between the second last name and 'and' or '&'.
Franklin, Gibson, Merkel-Stoll, Neufelt, and Vergara-Yiu (1996) found that . . .
[later in the report or essay] Franklin et al. (1996)
. . . found few differences (Franklin, Gibson, Merkel-Stoll, Neufelt, & Vergara-Yiu, 1996).
[Later] . . . confirmed (Franklin et al., 1996).

Six or more authors:
Use Smith et al. (1995) in text, but you need *all* the names and initials in your reference list. The exception in-text is where this would be confusing if there was another reference that also contracted to Smith et al. In such a situation, give the minimum number of authors needed to avoid confusion, e.g., Smith, Jones, et al. (1995).

Multiple citations:
If citing more than one work by the same author, put them in chronological order. If published in the same year, identify them by lower case letters after the date both in the text and in your reference list.
. . . was demonstrated (Jones, 1991, 1993).
Thorson and Powell (1992a, 1992b) showed that . . .

Two or more works within the same parentheses:
When referring to several works within the same parentheses, order them in the same order they would appear in the reference list, that is, in alphabetical order of the first author, or if there are two by the same author, then in chronological order.

Several researchers have argued that . . . (Faelli & Carless, 1999; Gallois, Callan, & McKenzie-Palmer, 1992; Gebart-Eaglemont, 1994; Ward & Kennedy, 1992).

are accurately describing the work of the original author, not taking someone else's word for it. However, if your institution does not have an extensive periodical collection, or time or library policy does not permit you to obtain copies from other libraries, a small number of secondary sources are usually acceptable in first and second year.

Appropriateness of sources Since you are reporting a scientific study, your sources should be appropriately scientific. Your marker will *not* be impressed by references in a lab report to such publications as *Reader's Digest* or *Women's Weekly*! I'll have more to say on this topic in Chapter 6 when discussing material from the Internet.

Quotations You should try to avoid directly quoting other people's work. The exceptions are where you can't say it in your own words without using many more words than the original; you can't paraphrase it without distorting the meaning; it is so memorable that you can't capture the meaning in a paraphrase; or you need an acknowledged expert to back up a conclusion. Given the general quality of writing of many published reports, these occasions are very few and far between.

If you do use a quote, ensure that it is brief. Enclose the quote in quotation marks (' . . . '), and include the page number after the year in the in-text reference, so your reader can check to see if you've quoted the author correctly and in context. For example, 'the key ingredient to genius is productivity – large in volume, extraordinary in longevity' (Albert, 1975, p. 144).

If you feel that you really do have to include a quotation longer than 40 words, it should be presented as an indented paragraph, without quotation marks. For example:

Many people favour Pope's (1980) definition of love:

> A preoccupation with another person. A deeply felt desire to be with the loved one. A feeling of incompleteness without him or her. Thinking of the loved one often, whether together or apart. Separation frequently evokes feelings of genuine despair or else tantalising anticipation of reuniting. Reunion is seen as bringing feelings of euphoric ecstasy or peace and fulfilment. (p. 4)

Avoid lengthy quotations It is much better to paraphrase them in your own words, and acknowledge their source. This demonstrates that you understand what the author was saying, and will be much more likely to impress your marker than large undigested chunks of other people's work! For the same reason, you should avoid having more than one or two quotations in any essay or lab report, even if they are brief. If you have a lot of quotations, it is not always clear to your marker that you understand what has been said, and you will lose marks.

A last word on plagiarism Be careful when paraphrasing another author's work. Don't just change a few words around or replace them with synonyms. This is just a subtler form of plagiarism. Try to understand what was meant and say it in your own style, and still acknowledge the source. Those students who convince their marker that they really understand what they have read and are not just regurgitating someone else's work are the ones who get the better marks.

2.7 Proofreading and redrafting

Always proofread drafts A distressing number of lab reports are handed in for marking without being proofread. This behaviour is throwing marks away. It indicates to the marker that you do not care very much about the presentation of the report. Apart from minor evidence of carelessness, such as typographical errors (typos), it is not unusual to find some rather strange expression in undergraduate reports or the misuse of psychological jargon. It is important that your work could be read by a non-professional who would then understand what you did and why. I will say something in the next chapter about the use of a friend, sister or mother, to operate as what Kidder and Judd (1986) call an 'unclarity detector'. If they find that something that you have written is unclear, don't argue with them, or try to clarify the problem verbally. If they have read it conscientiously, they are always right – by definition the writing is unclear. Even if their suggestions for fixing it are wrong or stupid, as detectors of lack of clarity, readers are never wrong.

You should not be shy about asking fellow students to do this for you, as long as they are not writing the same lab report or essay. Of course, this implies that you should also be prepared to do the same for them. This is essentially what happens in the real world of publishing. Writers usually get peer reviews before submitting their work for publication. Some students see their fellows as competitors, particularly third-year students. I find this upsetting and, at least in first and second year, inaccurate. Being prepared to give and receive criticism, and keeping that criticism focused on the writing, and not the writer, is good preparation for later work experience.

After proofreading, what then? Having received some constructive criticism, you need to start the long task of polishing and rewriting. Since essays are not constrained by the same conventions that lab reports are, you may find that an essay will need even more rewriting! Make sure your time management has allowed for this.

Time management Most assignments are set so that you have several weeks before they are due. You should make a timetable of what needs to be done, and do your best to stick to it. The checklists in section 4.11 (lab report) and in section 5.8 (essay) are good starting points. There are no foolproof guidelines, because students work at very different rates. However, experience has shown that students are less stressed if they get some writing done early. It is easier to correct and elaborate on something already written than to try to hold material in your head then write it all at once. I describe the steps involved in getting started in section 3.3 (pp. 36–40).

Relation between effort and grades Another complaint of many students is that they put an enormous amount of time and effort into their essay but did not get the grade they expected. Although generally speaking, the more drafts the better the grade, this assumes that the revised drafts *are* better than the earlier ones. Don't be like the job applicant who says they've had twenty years' experience, when in fact they've only had the same year of experience repeated twenty times! Redrafting your writing is hard work. Make sure that the concerns of your reviewer are really met in the next draft.

What to look for when redrafting The sort of things to look for when rewriting a draft are: is there a clear topic sentence in each paragraph, preferably at the start? Is there only one major point per paragraph? Do the paragraphs vary in length, without being either too short or too long? Avoid single-sentence paragraphs. A paragraph should not be longer than a page of double-spaced typing, and on average should be about half a page long. Are your sentences really sentences?

Not only should your drafts be read for clarity of argument and expression, but your final version should be proofread for typos or printing errors. The ease with which word processing programs allow you to cut-and-paste words, sentences or paragraphs leads to the possibility of all sorts of errors. If you can't get someone else to proofread the final version, leave it for a day and proofread it yourself. Do not be concerned about the appearance of a few patches of liquid paper or *neat* handwritten corrections on the final draft. Your reader will appreciate the care you have taken. Do not forget to keep a copy, either on disk or a photocopy. Submit the original, not the copy!

2.8 Some pet gripes of this author

Most markers will admit to being especially irritated by particular behaviours in the presentations of their students. These vary with the marker, and are often not of major importance in themselves. However, these behaviours are usually indicative of poor use of English, or poor proofreading, or both, and can be reasonably easily fixed. Although other markers will no doubt have additional gripes, here are some of my concerns with student essays and lab reports. If you avoid these, I believe that you will also avoid irritating other markers.

Incomplete sentences One of my pet gripes is when students make an assertion in one sentence, then follow it with a supposed sentence containing only a participle. For example: 'Bloggs (1993) found . . . to be the case. Thus proving Smith (1989) wrong.' That second sentence is *not* a sentence. It should be all one sentence, thus: 'Bloggs (1993) found . . . to be the case, thus proving Smith (1989) wrong.'

Similar words having different meanings Another gripe of mine is the misuse of 'effect' and 'affect', which are words you will frequently find yourself using in both essays and lab reports. They are easy to misuse because both can be used as either a verb or a noun. However, generally speaking 'affect' is used as a verb ('level of lighting affects visual acuity') except where it is used as a synonym for emotion or mood ('the procedure induced a positive affect'). In contrast, 'effect' is usually used as a noun ('the effect of level of self-esteem on . . .').

Unjustified conclusions One other misuse of language that irritates me is to start a sentence with 'therefore' when the sentence does not follow logically from what has been said before. 'Therefore' should only be used in drawing a conclusion from clearly stated pieces of evidence.

Commas How is your punctuation? Another of my gripes is the inappropriate placing of commas. For a bad example: 'Whereas, Price's (1982), study used only the Framlingham questionnaire to ascertain the score of Type A behaviour, the validity of that score is uncertain.' In this sentence, I'd leave out the first two commas. My advice regarding the placement of commas is: if in doubt, leave the comma out.

Apostrophes Many students seem unclear about the correct use of apostrophes ('). In formal writing such as essays and lab reports, you should never use an apostrophe for contractions. For example, write 'it is', never 'it's', and 'do not', never 'don't'. (My use of such contractions in this book is an example of trying to be didactic, but in a user-friendly way. Such a tone is inappropriate in an essay or lab report.) The acceptable use of apostrophes is to indicate possession. For almost all words, you simply add apostrophe s, as follows: 'Galligan's paper . . .', 'Each participant's response . . .', '. . . this study's results . . .', 'These people's opinions . . .'. This is true even when the word already ends with the letter s, as long as there is only one of them, for example 'Roberts's article . . .'. However, when the noun is already plural, simply put an apostrophe after the s, for example 'All participants' responses . . .', 'These studies' findings . . .'. The other tricky situation is the possessive of compound groups. In such cases, you should add the apostrophe to the last word only, as in: 'Walker and Broderick's (1999) argument was that . . .', 'Crowe and Casey's (1999) study found . . .', 'Fallon and Bowles's (1999) suggestion that . . .', 'Bates et al's (1999) finding was that . . .'. If you are still unsure of the use of the apostrophe, you can almost always reword the sentence to avoid the need for one. The first example above can be avoided by saying: 'It has been argued by Walker and Broderick (1999) that . . .'.

Spelling I tend to put a line through misspelled words in assignments I mark. I don't consciously take marks off for it, but since most students use word processors, and most word-processing packages have easy to use spell-checkers, it indicates to me a lack of care taken with the assignment. However, spell-checkers will not pick up words that are correctly spelt but wrongly used, such as 'their' and 'there' or 'affect' and 'effect.' This is where it is advantageous to have someone else as a proofreader. Many spell-checkers use

American spellings, and markers do not usually fuss about these. I have included as Appendix D a copy of Burdess's (1991) 1000 commonly misspelled words, so that even if you are not using a word processor you should be able to easily check your spelling.

Your tutor or lecturer will probably be able to easily call to mind other examples that bother her or him. While not of great significance in terms of marks, the presence of such irritants may just tip the balance to your disadvantage if the marker is judging whether the assignment is worthy of, say, a very high pass or a credit grade.

2.9 The physical presentation of your assignment

It is always best to present your assignment typed. Some institutions demand it, and you should check if your institution is one of them. In any case, a well-presented report allows the marker to concentrate on the content, allowing better communication between writer and reader. The library or the student union in many institutions have word processing facilities available for student use. Check them out! If circumstances force you to submit a handwritten report, take extra care to ensure that it is well spaced and legible, preferably printed. No matter how fair-minded your marker, if your report is difficult to read, then the message you intend to impart may not get across. A sloppily presented report indicates that you do not care much about the assignment. Would you like your marker to take as little care in marking it?

Typing, spacing, margins, page numbers The following suggestions may sound unduly simplistic, but too often they are ignored by undergraduates and can lead to unnecessary complications. Type on one side of the paper only. Unless your institution specifically says otherwise, always double-space your lines and leave a wide margin (at least 4 cm) on the left. This margin allows your marker to write comments at the points in your report where they are most relevant. Number your pages in the upper right hand corner. The Introduction of a lab report, or the beginning of the essay is page one, and does not need a number. Start including a number on page two. If by some mischance the pages are separated, or are carelessly assembled in the wrong order, it is immediately apparent and may save you marks. Use a 12-point serif font, such as Times New Roman. Such fonts are easier to read, and 12-point is the smallest easily read size for essays and reports.

Appendices There are no formal expectations about appendices, and I get conflicting advice from other academics, so check with your tutor or lecturer about their expectations. I recommend that for a lab report, you should include as Appendices all your raw data if you collected it yourself, or the summary sheet of the results if they are given to you. Also include all statistical calculations, even if they are only in rough note form. Including your calculations or computer printouts will allow your marker to check whether you have used appropriate statistics, and in the case of a purely mathematical mistake, will allow the marker to make appropriate allowances. If you are not sure whether something should be included as an Appendix or not, then do include it. The worst that will happen is that it will be ignored.

Essays do not normally require Appendices. The only exception might be if you have access to a rare or unusual document that would not be available to the average reader. In that case you could include it as an Appendix.

Getting advice Be aware that many lecturers will not read drafts of reports. Although it might well be a useful learning experience, resources are scarce enough without, in effect, marking things twice. Many of the questions that students ask their tutors could be easily answered by their fellow students. If you need advice, and cannot get satisfactory answers from your fellow students, by all means see your lecturer or tutor, but have specific questions ready. Do not be afraid to have them written down. Your lecturer or tutor will appreciate your forethought. Many institutions are setting up Discussion boards accessible over the Internet. Students can 'post' questions or comments, and tutors or lecturers can 'post' replies. These are a very effective means of communication, since you can access them at your convenience, as can the staff member, and it saves the staff member answering the same question many times, since any other student can read the questions and answers.

Submit in a folder? Check with your lecturer or tutor about whether your report should be in a folder. In any case, a report is much easier to mark if it is stapled only at the top left-hand corner. Avoid at all costs those folders where each page is in a separate sleeve. Taking pages out individually to write comments on them is guaranteed to try the fairmindedness of any marker! Make sure that your name, your tutor or lecturer's name, the subject and year level, and day and time of your class are clearly marked on the title page of your report, and also on the outside of your folder. There is an example on page 106.

Chapter 3

Laboratory reports – how do you start?

KEYWORDS
aims, dependent variable, experiment, extension, hypothesis, independent variable, manipulation, operationalisation, participant, placebo, replication, study, theory

IN THIS CHAPTER

The process of writing a lab report

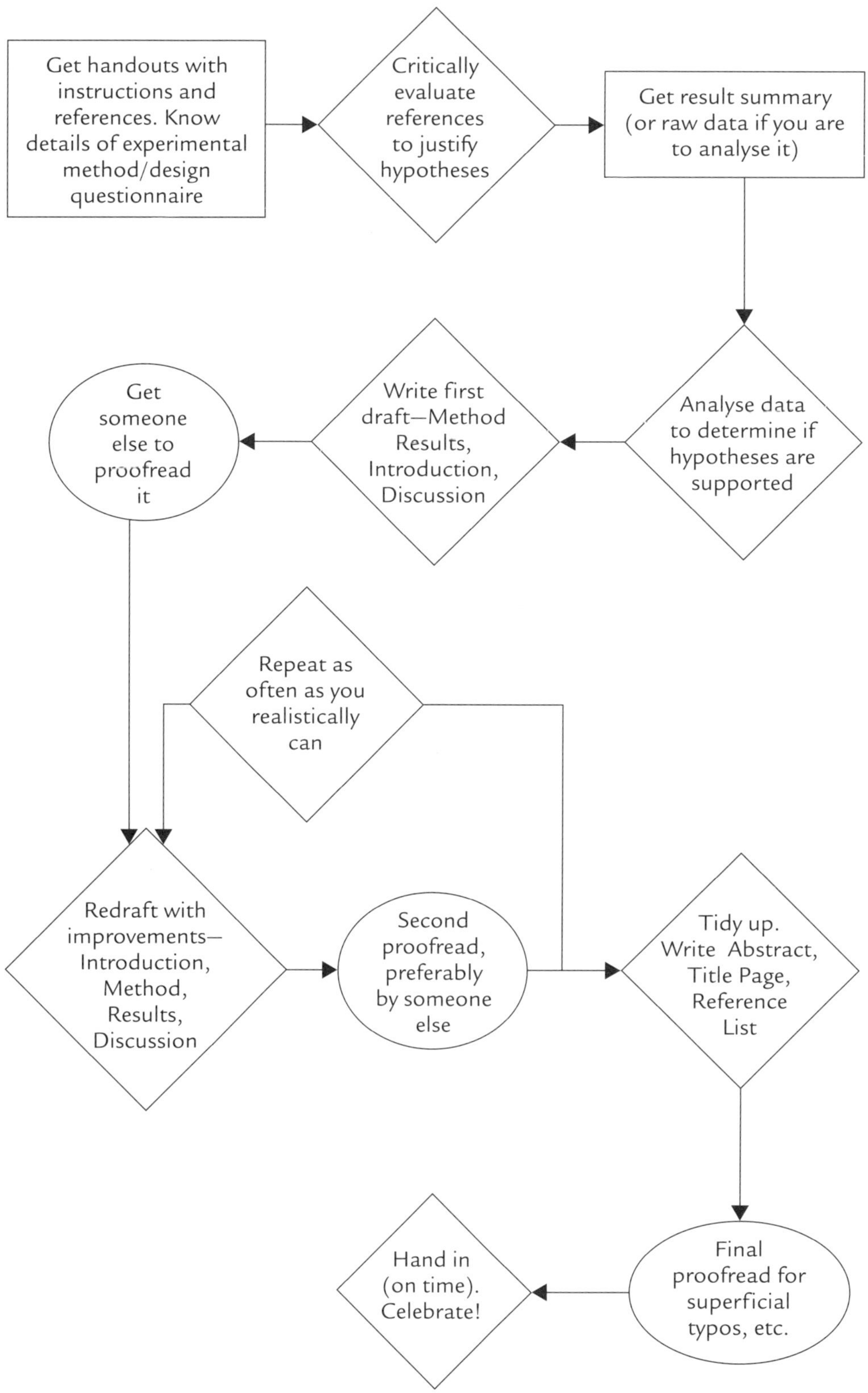

WITH ANY RESEARCH REPORT the starting point is 'What burning question do I want to answer?' From this starting point you need to look back to how you came to ask the question and also forward to the mechanics of answering it.

3.1 How to approach a lab report

There are two general approaches to writing lab reports. The first approach is to write the type of report you had in mind when you designed the study. Many psychologists, like other scientists, subscribe to the belief that advances in knowledge occur when a scientist, working from an existing body of knowledge, makes hypotheses about what would happen in particular situations. These hypotheses are then tested in an experiment, and the research report is written to publish the results of that experiment, indicating whether the original hypotheses were supported or not.

If science always worked in this linear fashion, you could write the report before you even did the study, just leaving blanks for the results, and having two Discussions, depending on whether the hypotheses were supported or not. In the real world of the social sciences, things do not tend to work so simply, because people's behaviour is rarely so straightforward and the concepts being examined are often difficult to define accurately.

The second approach to writing research reports is to write the report that makes the most sense after you've seen the results of your experiment. This approach means that you don't ignore interesting results that might not have been anticipated. Of course, if your original hypotheses are important tests of one theory over another, you wouldn't change the tone of your report to suit your results. On the other hand, many studies, especially in the area of people's social behaviour, begin with 'I wonder if . . .', and it makes good sense to re-orient your writing to the interesting things you have found. In this case, however, you are still expected to find theoretical justifications for your hypotheses in prior research. You may just have to look a bit harder to find them.

Besides, as an undergraduate, you will rarely be required to design your own studies. Typically, your lecturer or tutor will run an experiment with your class as participants, or will give you instructions on testing other people. The results will be collated by your lecturer or tutor and presented to your class to be used to test hypotheses. In this situation you might like, as Kidder and Judd (1986) suggest, to regard your data as uncut jewels. Your job is to cut and polish them, selecting and highlighting the best facets, and craft the best settings. In spite of the apparent lack of flexibility of the conventional format, good report writing does allow ample scope for the use of good judgment and skill.

3.2 How to begin

The first thing is to decide what your general research question is, and then derive one or more hypotheses from it. Remember that a hypothesis is a specific, testable prediction of what you expect to happen when you run the experiment. Once again there are two ways to jump, depending on whether the study has already been designed by your tutor or lecturer or whether you are designing the study.

3.2.1 Studies designed by the psychology department

Many of the lab reports you will have to write will be reports on studies which are already designed. You will have been a participant in the study run by your tutor or lecturer, or will have been given instructions on how to run the study on a participant or participants of your choosing. You will therefore be aware of what was actually done. However, when you come to write up the report, *you are expected to do so as if it was you who designed and ran the whole study, not your tutor or lecturer*. Keep in mind, however, the need for objective writing and the avoidance of personal pronouns.

Read the major reference It is not unusual for these studies to be replications of those that earlier researchers have published. That is, they are studies that exactly follow the procedures and materials used by an earlier researcher. You will be referred to the journal article where the report originally appeared, and possibly to other related articles. First read the relevant section in your textbook for an overview of the area and as a guide for other potentially useful references. Then carefully read the article to be replicated and any others given to you, and see what their authors hypothesised, and whether their hypotheses were supported. Read them critically. Before you get to the Method section of any particular report, ask yourself, 'If I had to do an experiment to test their hypotheses, what would I do?' Then, when you've read the rest of the report, ask 'Does the Method actually test the hypotheses?', 'Would I draw the same conclusion from those results?', 'If not, how would I interpret them?', 'Is there any other explanation that would give the same results?' Make notes as you go. The sort of notes you should make will be dealt with later in this chapter.

Aims and hypotheses On the basis of these questions and your answers to them, decide what the general aim of your study should be, and what specific results you expect to obtain when you replicate the experiment. Typically, you can expect the results to be similar, especially if the original participants were also university students. However, it may be that there is something different about the situation in which you ran the experiment. Perhaps yours is a different culture to that of the original, or you had participants who are a different gender or age to the original ones, or you made some other experimental manipulation. You might therefore expect a different result.

Write your expectations in concrete and specific terms. These are your hypotheses. Table 3 shows possible aims and hypotheses. Please do not confuse the two. Aims are general statements of the goals of the study, while hypotheses are specific predictions of what you expected to happen.

Further references If other journal articles are recommended by your tutor or lecturer, read them to see if they support or do not support the findings of the major article. If no other articles are specifically referred to, look at the reference lists of the major article and see if any of the reports there seem to be relevant. Look especially for articles published in journals that you know are held in the periodicals section of your library. Also look at later issues of the journals that the first article appeared in and see if there are more recent articles on the same subject. The assessor of your lab report will be impressed if you have looked for and found other publications and have made relevant and sensible comments about them.

Table 3

Examples of Possible Aims and Their Corresponding Hypotheses

Aim:
The aim of this study was to confirm that a conformity effect occurs during group discussion.

✓ **Hypothesis:**
It was predicted that the range of opinions would be reduced after group discussion, compared with the pre-discussion range of opinions.

Aim:
The present study aimed to measure the differences in the ability of subjects of varying ages to recall lists of digits.

✓ **Hypothesis:**
It was hypothesised that for children and adolescents, the number of digits able to be recalled would increase with the age of the subject.

Aim:
The aim of the current study was to produce the serial-position effect with free recall of a list of words.

✓ **Hypothesis:**
The hypothesis was that words at the beginning and end of the list would be recalled by more subjects than words in the middle of the list.

Note: The aims are general statements of intent, but the hypotheses are worded in terms of the specific variables being measured.

report will be impressed if you have looked for and found other publications and have made relevant and sensible comments about them.

You will also find books referred to in reference lists. These are often hard to get hold of, and it is not usually cost-effective in terms of your time to chase around looking for them. Use them if you can get them easily, since they often have overviews of the subject you are interested in, but journal articles are usually more accessible and up to date.

Databases There are also a number of reference materials to use when searching for information on a particular subject in psychology. Your library probably has copies of *Social Sciences Citation Index* and *Psychological Abstracts*. Both are indexed by subject and author and are important resources for psychology students. Many libraries now have a CD-ROM program called *PsychInfo* which allows you to search for psychological publications from 1887 on, though you should generally confine yourself to recent articles. If you have access to *PsychInfo*, you will find it is extremely useful in tracing articles by author, subject or keyword. Depending on the number of students at your institution, there may be restrictions on access to the CD-ROM program, and you may have to be satisfied with the printed versions. However, many journals are now becoming available on the Internet. Ask your librarian to help you become familiar with any of these resources.

Taking notes on references You can make notes in a number of different ways about the materials you read. One way is to photocopy the relevant articles, read them carefully, and highlight the most important parts, such as hypotheses, participants, the design of the experiment and conclusions about whether the hypotheses were supported or not. The danger with photocopying everything is that you are tempted to highlight anything even vaguely interesting. This approach does not usually sufficiently reduce the information to manageable amounts, and increases the dangers of plagiarism. A good method is to be strict about highlighting only material immediately relevant to your own study.

Another very effective way of making notes about articles you read is to use 12.5 cm × 7.5 cm cards, which you can get from your bookstore or a stationery supply shop. Using cards saves you money because you are not photocopying everything, but it requires you to spend a lot of time in the library, since periodicals usually cannot be borrowed. Write the source on the back of the card, precisely as it will appear in your Reference list (see Chapter 4). On the front, briefly summarise the relevant parts of the study using the major subheadings: type of participants, what was done, what was found, what was concluded, what you think is a better or different interpretation and anything that the author omitted, or questions the study raised. Assemble these cards in categories depending on whether they support or do not support the study you are replicating; or in any other sort of order that seems logical to you.

Yet another way of making notes about relevant journal articles is to use one of the flexible databases on your computer. Many students find that having to write the relevant information on cards or type it into a computer is a more effective way of absorbing information than simply highlighting a photocopy. This system also allows you to cut and paste references from one document to the other and so saves some typing time. If you have access to a bibliographic program such as Endnotes or Procite this will make producing a good reference list much easier.

3.2.2 Studies you design

Your approach to preparing for a lab report will be a little different if you have the freedom to design your own study. If you have this freedom, first look at what constraints are placed on you. What is the general area you are expected to work in? How much time do you have? Are you expected to test something experimentally, or is a survey study acceptable?

Once you have decided on the scope and type of study, ask yourself what question or questions you want answered. What answers would you expect? Then have a look through some recent journals in that subject area to see what other researchers have done. Look at *PsychInfo* or *Psychological Abstracts* under the subject area. If any of these articles look interesting, look at their reference sections for clues to similar works. Read and make notes on anything that looks as if it is relevant to what you want to do, especially if it supports what you expect to happen in your study (but don't ignore contrary results, they'll be handy if your hypotheses are not supported!). Make notes as mentioned above, and finally decide what you really predict will happen from the study as you conceive it.

The hypotheses need to be justified on the basis of prior research. Your study design will follow from the way you word your hypotheses. The hypotheses need to be operationalised in such a way that it is practical to collect the data. That is, if the study is to be a questionnaire study, the scales used need to be available. If the study is an experimental task, the facilities need to be available, and a means of getting participants to become involved. In my experience, it is unlikely that you will be expected to design and run your own study in the first couple of years of an undergraduate degree in psychology. When you are expected to do this, you should be given a good deal of guidance. If you feel you don't have enough guidance, ask for assistance.

3.2.3 All studies

It is important that your hypotheses are specific and concrete. They must be expressed in terms that make it clear how you are going to measure the theoretical concepts you are interested in. Sometimes it is hard to operationalise hypotheses; that is, to formulate precise, concise, testable statements of what your theory would predict. You may find, if you are comparing groups of people, that it is useful to draw up a matrix of the independent and dependent variables. You can then be more specific in saying what you predict will happen. Such a matrix is illustrated in Table 4.

Table 4

Example of a Matrix of Independent and Dependent Variables

	Age (Independent)	
	Younger	Older
Gender (Independent)	Reaction time	Reaction time
Female		
Male	Reaction time	Reaction time

Note: Reaction time is the dependent variable. Age and gender are independent variables.

Independent variables Remember, independent variables are those that are hypothesised to have some causal influence on whatever behaviour is being studied. They are usually varied by you, the experimenter, selecting categories of the variable such as gender (male and female); daily alcohol consumption (low and high); or age (adolescent and middle-aged). Sometimes they are specifically manipulated by you, the experimenter, such as drug dose (low, high, placebo). Sometimes the independent variable is simply allowed to vary, such as a score on intelligence or satisfaction with body image. Independent variables can therefore refer to different groups of subjects or to different conditions of testing.

Dependent variables Dependent variables are what you are interested in measuring. They are called 'dependent' variables because you are hoping that the value of the dependent variable *depends* on your manipulation of the independent variables. The exercise on the next page gives you some examples of conditions and asks you to decide which are independent and which are dependent variables. Try yourself out on this.

As mentioned above, it is unlikely that you will have to design and run your own study before your second, or even your third, year of psychology, so this book will not address such details. I will assume that you have either been a participant in a study run by your tutor or lecturer, or have tested one or more participants using instructions from your tutor or lecturer. You will therefore know how the study was conducted and will be in possession of the results of the study in the form of raw data, or perhaps some form of summary data.

3.2.4 Research ethics

Any substantial psychological study should be approved by your departmental or university ethics committee. Studies run by the department on you as a participant should already have been approved. If you are asked to collect data from other people,

Exercise

Following are some very brief statements about the design of some studies. Read each statement and identify which is the independent variable and which is the dependent variable. Answers are on page 122.

1 The effect of severity of initiation on liking for a group.

2 Group size and conformity in response to group pressure.

3 Time continuously on target as a function of distribution of practice.

4 Type of association in word pairs and recall memory for lists of them.

5 Self-rating of nausea after administration of drug, placebo, or no treatment.

6 Driving ability and alcohol or cannabis intoxication.

7 The relation of childhood training in independence to achievement motivation.

8 Level of anxiety and preference for waiting alone or with others for an experiment involving electric shock.

9 The effects of room temperature and distracting music on accuracy of typing.

10 Variations in heart rate and blood pressure in viewing either a violent or non-violent film sequence.

this should also have been approved. In later years when you are expected to design and run your own research, your research plan will have to be submitted to the ethics committee for approval. The purpose of this is ultimately to protect the participants of the study: you and your fellow students and any other participants in the studies.

There are four cardinal rules of research ethics. The first is that participants should be informed of what is expected of them, and freely give their consent to participate. The second is that participants should be told (and it should be true!) that they can withdraw from the study at any time, without penalty. Third, information obtained from participants should be kept confidential, and individuals should not be able to be identified from what is reported about the study. Finally, the overriding aim is: Do no harm! That is, participants should suffer no ill effects from taking part in the study. If for any reason participants do suffer distress, mechanisms should be in place to deal with them. These mechanisms usually exist within the resources of the psychology department.

As a participant in a study, all these rules apply to you. You may feel somewhat pressured to take part as a student who will later write up the report of the study. However, lab reports are an important part of a psychology major, and being a participant in studies lets you discover how participants in your studies may feel if you get to the stage of running your own. It also gives you an idea of the ambiguities in responding that participants in studies encounter. If answering questionnaires or taking part in studies is a turn-off, you might wish to reconsider your ambition to become a psychologist. Having said that, if you genuinely and sincerely feel uncomfortable about a particular study, you are at liberty not to participate as a subject, and your tutor or lecturer should respect that right. However, you *are* still expected to write the lab report based on the study – that is part of your course requirement. A good many undergraduate studies are based on data collected in questionnaires. You will be informed of the general content of these, and you can choose to hand in the questionnaire or not. By their nature, questionnaires are usually anonymous, and so the confidentiality rule is met, but if you are the only 56-year-old male in the class, and are concerned about confidentiality, do not feel obliged to hand in the questionnaire!

In situations where the study is an experimental task, if you feel uncomfortable about being involved as a participant, it is usually possible to be allocated as a support person – either a timer, a counter or an 'instructor'. If you are feeling distressed or pressured, you should raise the question with your tutor or lecturer, since others in the class may feel the same, but be inhibited about speaking out. In my experience it is rare that a classroom study is this uncomfortable for students. In the unlikely case that you feel that your concerns are not treated seriously, talk to the coordinator of the course. I say 'unlikely' because the tutor or lecturer is usually more concerned about ethics than most students.

The rules become even more important if you are collecting data from people outside the university. If you are interviewing a child, you will probably be given fairly strict instructions about obtaining permission from the child's parents, gaining the child's confidence, and discontinuing the interview if the child becomes uncomfortable. People are more important than your study! Such experiences of having to meet the concerns of people in the real world are good practice for anyone wishing to become either a psychologist or a market researcher, and will allow you to view with a critical or perhaps an admiring eye, some of the research you will read.

I'd be surprised if you were not introduced to the ethics of research very early in your undergraduate course. Such an introduction may mention some possible exceptions to the rules I've mentioned, but they are very few and far between and unlikely to apply to undergraduate studies. The Australian Psychological Society encapsulates its expectations of the ethical behaviour of psychologists, both as researchers and practitioners, in a small booklet called *Code of Ethics* (October, 1997) available from the Society.

3.3 Where to go from here?

What belongs in each section of the report will be dealt with at some length in Chapter 4. In the present section I deal with the general process of writing the lab report, assuming you have already participated in some way in running the study and have some resulting data.

Hypotheses As a participant it is unlikely that you were aware of the actual hypotheses at the time the study was run. It is also common practice for you as an experimenter not to be told the hypotheses at the time you test some other participant. The hypotheses will become clear from your reading about the study you are replicating, or from other reading, and from reflecting on what the study actually tested.

By deciding on your hypotheses you have already largely determined the shape of your report. Your Introduction must consist of a logical argument for why you have made those particular predictions. Your Method must describe a study that does actually test your predictions. In your Results section you need report only those results that are relevant to your hypotheses. Your Discussion must say whether or not your hypotheses were supported, then interpret them and discuss their implications.

Get something down in writing You should begin by writing an outline of the structure of your report. The best lab reports are thoroughly planned. A good starting point is to jot down the answers to the following questions:

- Why is this area worth studying?
- Which previous study or studies is this one like, and why?
- What did previous studies find, and am I predicting similar findings?
- What other studies relate specifically to my predictions?
- What is the overall aim of my study?

I use the first person pronouns here to reinforce the pretence that you have designed the study. Remember, however, to be more objective when actually writing the report. The answers to these questions will form the Introduction to your study. The Method section is an answer to the questions:

- Who were the participants?
- How was the study conducted, and what materials were used?
- What actually happened?

To prepare to write the Results section, the overall question you need to ask is:

- What results are specifically relevant to my hypotheses?

Finally, in preparing the Discussion, you need to answer these questions:

- Do my results support my hypotheses?
- What do my results actually mean?

- How do they relate to the previous studies I've mentioned?
- What are the implications of my results for real-world situations?
- How could my study have been improved?

The answers to all the above questions need to be tidied up, expanded and separated into the conventional sections of the lab report, but they are the essentials of the report.

It is often difficult for students to grasp just which elements of a study are the important ones, especially if it has not been designed by the student. A plan helps to sort out your priorities. The next step is to start writing the report itself. Often just getting started is the most difficult part. You should get something down in writing as soon as possible. You can later edit, rewrite, expand and tidy it up.

Length of each section Students frequently ask how long each section of the report should be. There are no formal rules about this, but a rule of thumb is that the Introduction should be about a third of the length of the total report. Although the lengths can vary with the type of study, the remaining sections are often roughly equal to each other in length.

Word limits Typically, students have trouble keeping the length of their reports within the word limit. Most markers do not have the time to actually count the words, so it is not necessary to agonise over 40 or 50 words in excess. However, writing to a word limit is a skill you are expected to learn, and one highly valued in the professional world, so anything more than about 10% over the word limit will almost certainly lose you marks.

How much time should I spend on it? A common question asked by students is: 'How much time should I spend on a lab report?' There is no simple answer, because students' speed of working is so variable. A glib answer is to ask in return 'What proportion of my assessment is it worth compared with other assessable pieces of work?' If the lab report is worth 10% of your annual assessment, and an exam is worth 30%, you might be expected to put in a third of the time you spend studying for the exam. On the other hand, if you tend to cram for the exam at the last minute, this might not be good advice. Perhaps it should be a third as much time as you *should* spend studying for the exam!

What do I have to do to get a pass? Experience indicates that the average student needs to satisfactorily complete the following tasks in order to get a grade of 'high pass' for her or his report:

- Obtain sufficient relevant references (usually at least as many more as you've already been given, but some institutions expect a minimum of five in the first year, so check with your tutor or lecturer), read them and decide on hypotheses that your study does actually test.

- Calculate the appropriate statistics and decide if your hypotheses are supported or not.
- Write an outline of your report as indicated above.
- Write a first draft, which may be pretty rough.
- Get that draft read by another person, such as a friend, mother or sister who is not a psychology student. This is to ensure that your Introduction is a coherent argument for your hypotheses, that the Method and Results are understandable, and that the Discussion makes sense of what the results have told you.
- On the basis of their comments about whether it makes sense, add, subtract or otherwise alter your draft.
- Type it up.
- Get the final presentation proofread and tidied up.

Re-drafts You should *never* submit the first draft of any written piece of assessment for marking if you are serious about your work. The chances of producing even a sentence that is well written the first time are vanishingly small, let alone an entire report. An average student can improve her or his work by redrafting the work more than just once. How often you do that depends on how quickly you work, how important a good mark is to you, and how patient your proofreader is. However, the process of reviewing and redrafting is subject to the law of diminishing returns, which says that you have to put a lot more work in each time to get only a slightly better mark. Still, with thoughtful redrafting, even an average student can lift her or his mark each time it is redrafted.

Proofreading If you do not have the luxury of someone else as a proofreader, time your work so that you leave 24 hours between writing something and proofreading it yourself. It is very easy in the heat of creation to read what you meant to say instead of what you have actually written, and so overlook what may be quite gross errors of expression or logic. Your assessor can mark only what you have written, not what you meant to write!

Time management I partially addressed this in section 2.7. Although it is easier said than done, plan your time so that you allow more than you need. University timetables dictate that you will have assignments in several subjects due at the same time. Murphy's Law suggests that if you leave everything until the last minute, the word processor will choose that time to have a fatal breakdown, or the dog will chew up your final draft just as you sit down to type it up. Consequently, time your work to leave at least 48 hours between getting it finished and handing it in. That way, if there are any catastrophes, you do have some time up your sleeve in order to correct their effects.

Space your work time so that it can be done in several small chunks. Cooperate with other students to minimise the hassles of obtaining references from the library.

Start early enough so that if you have to get advice from staff you can do so during their consultation times. Most student consultations with staff seem to revolve around statistics. You should have tackled these early on. Asking questions about statistical problems at the last minute indicates that your planning is bad, and tests the fairmindedness of your tutor or lecturer, who probably got where he or she is by being on top of their assignments when they were in your shoes!

Extensions Although institutions will grant extensions of time for genuinely unavoidable difficulties, this does not generally include pressure of other work. Be prepared to document any problems you have. If your printer fails at the last minute, be prepared to show your tutor or lecturer your last draft or the disk with the final version on it.

Copies of your report or essay Always keep a copy of your final submission. Most institutions have a policy that assignments gaining very high or very low marks are to be double-marked. Hopefully yours will be the former, but the policy results in reports being handed on by one staff member to another, and so may occasionally be misplaced.

In the next chapter I give detailed advice about the various sections of a lab report, including examples of the conventions for writing each part.

CHAPTER 4

Sections of a Laboratory report

KEYWORDS
aims, apparatus, data, degrees of freedom, dependent variable, descriptive statistics, design, hypothesis, independent variable, inferential statistics, participant, post hoc, proof/prove, sample, scale, secondary source, significance level, statistic, variable

IN THIS CHAPTER

THE PARTS OF THE report, in the order that they should appear in your final version, are as follows:

- Title Page and Abstract
- Introduction
- Method
- Results
- Discussion
- References
- Appendices

That is the order in which they will be treated in this chapter. However, you may find it easier to draft them in some other order. For instance, the Method and Results sections are very largely clerical exercises, since they report straightforward factual material. The Method describes who the participants were, what materials were used, and the procedure that was followed. The Results section describes the data you collected, states what statistical methods were used to test your hypotheses and the mathematical results of those tests. You may find it easier to write these two sections first, although you will, of course, have to decide on your hypotheses and do the appropriate statistical calculations to test those hypotheses before you can do so.

4.1 Title page and Abstract

Title page The title page should contain a relatively brief title that encapsulates the essence of what the research does. In the academic world, many important reference sources, such as *Current Contents*, list only the titles of articles. It is critical that your title indicates the central research question. This task is best done if you can include the independent and dependent variables in your title. Some real examples of article titles are shown in Table 5. The title should be centred horizontally on the page, and about a third of the way down the page. Your name should also be centred, about two lines below the title.

Your tutor's name, your subject name and code, the due date, and the day and time of your class should be at the bottom of the page, flush with the left margin. One commonly used layout is shown in Table 6. Check with your tutor or lecturer whether the conventions at your university require anything different.

Abstract This follows the title page, and has a page to itself. As you will learn from searching databases like *PsychInfo*, the Abstract needs to contain sufficient information to convince a searcher that the report is worth reading. Since it is restricted in length to a maximum of 120 words, it has to pack a lot of information into a small space. It is critically important that the Abstract contains information about: (a) the aim(s) of

Table 5

Some Titles of Published Articles by Australasian Psychologists ✓

The Effects of Participation and Presentation Media on the Eyewitness Memory of Children. (Bates, Ricciardelli & Clarke, 1999)
On Feeling Good and Being Rude: Affective Influences on Language Use and Request Formulations. (Forgas, 1999)
Perceptions of a Media Campaign: The Role of Social Identity and the Changing Intergroup Context. (Duck, Terry & Hogg, 1998)
Predicting Memory Performance of Very Old Men and Women: Contributions from Age, Depression, Activity, Cognitive Ability, and Perceptual Speed. (Luszcz, Bryan & Kent, 1997)
Blur and Contrast as Pictorial Depth Cues. (O'Shea, Govan & Sekuler, 1997)
Social Evaluation of Fair and Unfair Allocators in Interpersonal and Intergroup Situations. (Platow, O'Connell, Shave & Hanning, 1995)
Adult Attachment, Emotional Control, and Marital Satisfaction. (Feeney, 1999)
Leadership, Managerial Performance and 360-degree Feedback. (Carless, Mann & Wearing, 1998)
Culture and Language: The Case of Cultural Dimensions and Personal Pronoun Use. (Kashima & Kashima, 1998)

the study; (b) the participants; (c) some overview of what was done; (d) whether the hypotheses were supported; and (e) what was concluded.

You will find it advantageous to write this section last. By then you will have written about what it was you were testing (Introduction), how you did it and to whom (Method), what you found (Results), and what you concluded (Discussion). The Abstract is a precis or summary of these aspects of your report. For an undergraduate report, the Abstract should be on a separate page. The heading should be the word Abstract, in upper case (capital) and lower case (small) letters centred across the page. The Abstract itself should be a single paragraph of double-spaced typing, containing a maximum of 120 words, centred vertically on the page and flush with the left margin.

It is customary to begin with a sentence stating the aim of the study. This is followed by the number and type of participants. Only include information sufficient to inform the reader about those characteristics of the participants that are relevant to the

Table 6

Example of a Typical Title Page

The Effect of Group Discussion on the Polarisation of Attitudes in Group and Individual Decision-making.

Kathy Smith

Submitted as a Psychology 201 Practical Report
Due date: 6 October
Tutor: Alison Roberts
Class: Wednesday, 10:30–12:30

conclusions drawn, and mention whether they were university students or a community sample. Age or gender need only be mentioned if they affect either the research question or the representativeness of the sample. These opening statements are followed by a very brief overview of what was actually done, that is, the experimental method. In the interests of brevity it is then best to state that 'the hypotheses that . . . (whatever your hypotheses were) were (or were not) supported'. A final sentence can then be written stating the conclusions that you drew from these results. Some examples are given in Table 7.

You will find it useful to look at some of the major journals for examples of Abstracts. Try *Journal of Personality and Social Psychology*, *Child Development* and *Sex*

Table 7

Examples of Abstracts

This study explored the relationship between Type A behaviour, stress and task difficulty. Participants were 30 undergraduates selected from a larger study at a metropolitan university, whose stress levels were measured before and after a pattern-matching task which was either unpressured or deliberately designed to provoke Type A behaviours by providing an environment that was achievement-oriented, time-pressured, and self-esteem threatening. Self-reported Type A behaviours were also measured. The hypothesis that people higher in Type A behaviour are more stressed during a more pressured task was supported, though they were not more stressed in general. It was concluded that measurement of Type A behaviour needs to focus on all aspects of this behaviour pattern not just the time-urgency.

This study examined 'hoped for' selves across the age range, and their relationships with current well-being. Two hundred and ninety four introductory psychology students and their acquaintances responded to a survey about hoped for, and feared selves, and psychological well-being. Occupational hoped-for selves were most frequently reported, possibly reflecting the predominantly young sample and the current economic conditions. The area of family was also considered important. Contrary to previous findings, capability of achieving hoped-for selves did not differ across age groups, nor did type of hoped-for self differ depending on current well-being. It was concluded that, although the study needs to be replicated with a sample of more diverse age, most people report being capable of achieving hoped-for selves.

The aim of this study was to test whether there was a bias towards drawing left-facing profiles, and if so, whether this is affected by handedness. Under counterbalanced conditions, 431 undergraduate students were requested to draw a person's head in profile, to report, from memory, which way the Queen's head faced on a 20-cent coin, and to draw the head side of a 20-cent coin from memory. Results indicated that a substantial majority of people drew a left-facing profile, regardless of handedness. When asked which way the Queen's head faced on a coin, they answered at no better than chance levels. It was concluded that a left-facing drawing bias exists which is unrelated to visualisation or handedness.

The purpose of this study was to test the hypothesis of an inverted-U relationship between stress and arousal and performance on judgment of perceptual accuracy. The sample consisted of 211 female and 89 male undergraduate university students who judged the accuracy of repeated presentations of the horizontal-vertical illusion, and reported their level of stress and arousal using a popular checklist. Results indicated that, contrary to expectations, there was no relationship between arousal and perceptual accuracy. It was concluded that perceptual arousal did not appear to be related to stress or arousal for this rather simple type of judgment, but that further studies should examine the effect of differing levels of task complexity.

Roles for areas that you may encounter in your very early studies. Later you may want to look at journals such as *Journal of Experimental Psychology* for Abstracts of studies in the areas of cognition and perception.

4.2 Introduction

By the time you sit down to write the Introduction, you should have read enough previous research to have decided on your hypotheses, tested them with the appropriate statistics, and decided what the results told you. You need to write the Introduction as if you were the researcher who designed the study. *You* know what the report is about, and the Introduction should lead the reader along the path you took to decide why you tested the particular hypotheses you did test.

You should begin the Introduction on a new page. *Do not* give the heading 'Introduction'. The location of the Introduction tells the reader what it is. The page on which the Introduction begins is also not numbered. Page numbering begins with '2' at the top right-hand corner of the second page of the Introduction. Some institutions suggest that you repeat the title at the top of the page on which the Introduction begins, but this is not the usual convention. Ask your tutor or lecturer whether this style is expected.

Opening sentences The purpose of an Introduction is to explain why you have undertaken your study, and to lead logically to why you expect whatever you hypothesise. It is (surprise!) an exercise in communication, and for that reason should be written in English prose, not psychological jargon. You should *not* leap straight into the middle of your research problem or theory. Instead you should lead the general reader step by step through your reasoning. Kidder and Judd (1986) put it nicely when they suggest that you open with a statement about human behaviour, not the behaviour of behavioural scientists or their research.

Do not allow this general statement to degenerate into cliché. Markers are not impressed by opening statements such as 'Ever since humanity came down from the trees, psychologists have been interested in . . .'! However, the behaviour being studied ought to be relevant in some way to the real world. You should be able to make a one- or two-sentence statement of this relevance. Some recent Australian examples are given in Table 8.

Define the area under study The initial general statement of the area under consideration should be followed by a statement of the theoretical framework that has generated the particular questions that you used for your study. You can usually find this in your textbook, and in the early part of the Introductions of the references you have been given. Do not make this part very long, but it is useful to define technical terms. Write it as if it were for an intelligent lay reader who is generally familiar with psychology, but not with the specific area you are reporting on. Be careful when

Table 8

Some Actual Examples of Opening Sentences

'Although school refusal can occur through the entire range of school years, it appears that school refusal in adolescence is a particularly challenging problem for mental health professionals.' (Rollings, King, Tonge, Heyne & Young, 1998, p. 87)

'Children are increasingly being called upon to give accounts of past experiences in contexts in which it is important that their accounts be as accurate and complete as possible. The typical finding from event memory research is that although even pre-school children can provide accurate free-recall accounts of past events, these accounts are much briefer than those of older children or adults [many references].' (Priestley, Roberts & Piper, 1999, p. 1006)

'The term *dual route theory* refers to a particular class of theories of visual word recognition and reading aloud. The defining feature of such theories is the postulate that there are two different procedures for converting print to speech: a dictionary look-up, or lexical procedure and a rule-bound, or nonlexical procedure . . .' (Rastle & Coltheart, 1999, p. 482)

'The perception and production of temporal patterns are fundamental abilities that are crucial for a wide range of [activities]. Yet there is still much that is not understood about some of the simplest temporal abilities. In particular, there is considerable disagreement concerning the mechanisms used to make duration and tempo judgments.' (McAuley & Kidd, 1998, p. 1786)

'The question of how best to characterize the psychological basis of children's addition problem-solving development has been intensely debated [references].' (Canobi, Reeve & Pattison, 1998, p. 882)

'Humans are exposed to manifold hazards: at the workplace, as commuters, at home and in their residential environment, during leisure activities, when travelling abroad, and so on. Risks might be induced by people's behaviour (e.g., driving, metal drilling, smoking, unprotected sex, climbing) or result from external agents (e.g., natural hazards such as earthquakes and bushfires, failure of technologies or industrial facilities, tropical diseases). In many situations, both oneself and others are placed at risk.' (Rohrmann, 1998, p. 105)

'A matter of some controversy in recent times has been the issue of the accuracy of psychologists' and psychiatrists' predictions of dangerousness, with current research reporting modest improvements in predictive accuracy (Borum, 1996).' (McMahon & Knowles, 1997, p. 207)

Note: I have put quotation marks around the above quotes, and given sources, including page numbers because they are direct quotes. You should summarise previous research in your own words, giving only the general reference at the end thus: (Slaughter, 1998). Avoid direct quotes to show that you understand the material.

defining terms, because many terms used in psychology have technical meanings somewhat different from their everyday use. For this reason, use a dictionary of psychology, not an ordinary dictionary. If you already know that you intend to major in psychology, a dictionary of psychology is a good investment. Most textbooks also have technical terms defined either in the body of the text or in a glossary.

Previous research Usually the studies that you encounter early in your undergraduate career will be replications or variations of previous research. This part of the Introduction should therefore consist of stating what previous researchers have done, what their theoretical positions are, and what they have concluded from their research. You should have a logical structure to the sequence in which you describe previous research. There are no strict rules for this, but one possibility is to describe the most general findings first, followed by descriptions of the findings in previous research that are specifically relevant to your hypotheses.

Describe all the relevant material from a particular piece of research in the one place. It is frustrating for your marker to read a paragraph about a specific study, then a couple of paragraphs about another one, then find more material about the first one. The reports that gain the best marks are those that follow a logical sequence.

You should be very selective about what you include. There is a temptation to write all you know about a previous study. Resist it! You need only include the material that is relevant to your subsequent hypotheses. Typically that means giving only the briefest overview of what the researcher did, to whom, and what was concluded from it. When reading previous research, you should have applied the principles of critical evaluation already described in section 2.2. In writing an overview of previous research, you should briefly describe the elements of that research in a way that indicates the quality of the evidence you are using to justify the hypotheses which you will make at the end of the Introduction. Some examples of summaries of previous findings are shown in Table 9. They are from recent publications by Australasian psychologists.

How much prior research should be included? Students often ask how much previous research they should include. It largely depends on the length allowed for the report. Check with your own tutor or lecturer, but most first-year lab reports are based on one or two specific references. However, you are expected to read beyond these central references. Second-year lab reports will often be assigned as many as five references, and you will certainly be expected to *read* at least as many more. A rule of thumb is that you will need to read at least as many more references as you have been given. You should *describe* enough previous research to justify the hypotheses you make, either to show that previous researchers have supported similar hypotheses, or to show that they have found sufficient data for you to deduce the predictions that your study tests.

It is common practice to read more references than you end up citing in your report. A good lab report will cite only *relevant* work and will indicate why it is relevant. The

Table 9

Some Real Examples of Summaries of Previous Research

'Longitudinal research by Markman and his colleagues has linked premarital communication to subsequent marital distress and divorce (see Markman, 1981; Markman & Hahlweg, 1993). Specifically, husbands' interactional negativity, emotional invalidation, and younger age of marriage were the best discriminators of marital dissolution.' (Sanders, Halford & Behrens, 1999, p. 61)

'Dawson, Filion, and Schell (1989, Experiment 1) reported an experiment which required participants to discriminate between relevant and irrelevant tone stimuli. Participants were instructed to count the number of longer-than-usual tones (7 s vs. 5 s) presented to one ear (task-relevant) and to ignore all tones presented to the other ear (task-irrelevant). Simultaneously with the tone-counting task, participants made a speeded response to a visual probe. Skin conductance responses during unprobed tone presentations were larger during task-relevant stimuli than during task-irrelevant stimuli.' (Neumann, Lipp & Siddle, 1998, p. 35)

'Zaitchik's (1990) now-famous series of studies examined children's understanding of misrepresentation by comparing preschoolers' performance on standard false belief tasks with their performance on a "false" photograph task. In one version of the photo task, a picture of an object was taken, then that object was replaced by a different object. Children were then asked to report which object was in the picture. Zaitchik's studies showed that preschool children tended to fail "false" photographic tasks at the same time that they failed false belief tasks.' (Slaughter, 1998, p. 321)

'Rusbult et al. (1993) used a combination of free-response data and multidimensional scaling to investigate relationship ideals. They found two dimensions: (a) superficial versus intimate and (b) romantic-traditional versus nontraditional.' (Fletcher, Simpson, Thomas & Giles, 1999, p. 73)

'Smolen, Spiegal, and Martin (1986) assessed individuals' reports of the frequency of their partners' infringements of their personal rights and their ability to respond assertively to those infringements. High rates of infringements by the partners, when combined with low personal assertion, were associated with low marital satisfaction and depression in both male and female partners.' (Halford, Bouma, Kelly & McD Young, 1999, p. 182)

'. . . Decety and Jeannerod (1995) recently used an ingenious task to control such demand characteristics . . . In this study, subjects were required to move a specified distance and pass through a gate within a virtual reality environment. Task difficulty was manipulated by varying the distance to be travelled and the width of the gate. The time necessary to complete each level of task difficulty in the virtual environment was compared to the time necessary to imagine performing the same task. They found that movement time varied as a logarithmic function of task difficulty for both the virtual and the imagined movements.' (Maruff et al., 1999, p. 379)

'. . . Fay et al. (1994) in a 3-year longitudinal follow-up of 72 children with [traumatic brain injury] and their matched controls found that parents, but not teachers, reported significantly more behavior problems in children with severe injuries.' (Kinsella, Ong, Murtagh, Prior & Sawyer, 1999, p. 116)

'Using latent trait analysis, Goldberg et al. (1987) found that two correlated dimensions of anxiety and depressive symptoms underlie neurotic disorders. Mackinnon et al. (1994) later extended this approach to the elderly.' (Christensen et al., 1999, p. 326)

Note: I have put quotation marks around the above quotes, and given sources, including page numbers because they are direct quotes. You should summarise previous research in your own words, giving only the general reference at the end thus: (Slaughter, 1998). Avoid direct quotes to show that you understand the material.

quality of what you include will indicate the appropriateness of your reading. It is better to cite a few well-chosen references than to have a long and unselective reference list. Reports will lose marks if the Introduction is little more than a collection of quotes and references.

Using examples In illustrating theoretical points or introducing technical terms it is important to use examples. The more abstract the theory the more important it is to use examples. Kidder and Judd (1986) give a very clear contrast in the following poor and good examples of opening statements:

✗ Poor: Festinger's theory of cognitive dissonance has received a great deal of attention during the past 15 years.

✓ Good: The individual who holds two beliefs that are inconsistent with one another may feel uncomfortable. For example, the person who knows that he or she enjoys smoking but believes it to be unhealthy may experience a discomfort arising from the disharmony or inconsistency between these two thoughts or cognitions. This feeling of discomfort has been called cognitive dissonance by social psychologist . . . Festinger (1957), who suggests that individuals will be motivated to remove this dissonance in whatever way they can . . . (p. 432).

Jargon Try to avoid jargon. Some people justify the use of jargon as necessary linguistic shorthand. However, an undergraduate lab report should be written for a more general readership, and without assuming expert knowledge on the part of the reader. Another reason for avoiding jargon is that your use of everyday language indicates to your marker that you understand the concepts that you are writing about.

Direct quotes For the same reason you should avoid lengthy direct quotes from your references. It is not always obvious from the use of quotations that you know what they mean. As already mentioned in section 2.6 (at pp. 17–18), rephrasing them in your own words (and acknowledging the source) shows your marker that you clearly understand what you are saying.

Introducing your own study Once you have reported what previous researchers have done in areas that are relevant to your hypotheses, it is time to say something about your own study. First you need a statement of general aims. An example is 'The present study will replicate Cross and Markus (1991) using a university student sample, but will also extend their work by asking (these other pertinent questions) . . .'. You can also add here any special or different treatments you used, or ways your study has been controlled for various problems. Such statements show that you are aware of the shortcomings of previous studies.

Hypotheses Finally, you need concise, specific, concrete hypotheses. These are explicit statements of what you expected to find. Your expectations should be justified by what you have already said about previous research. Do *not* use the abbreviations 'H_1' or 'H_0', and do *not* state or write about the null hypothesis. Each hypothesis should be stated operationally. That is, the variables should be defined in words that describe how they are actually measured. You should *not* number your hypotheses, or present them in bulleted note form. They should be written in flowing English prose, with all hypotheses in the same paragraph. Remember to write your hypotheses in the past tense. The study has already been run, or you would not be reporting on it. Therefore, say 'It was predicted that participants would . . .', or 'It was hypothesised that respondents would . . .'. You were given some examples in Table 3 of Chapter 3. There are some more examples, both good and not so good, in Table 10, which also illustrate what the difference is!

Length of sections There are no formal rules about the appropriate length of each section of a lab report, but a rough guide is that the Introduction should be about one-third of the length of the entire report.

4.3 Method

When writing your first draft of a lab report, it is easiest to write the Method first, because this section describes what was done and to whom. You will usually have been one of the participants of the experiment, or the experimenter, testing participants you

Table 10

Good and Poor Examples of Hypotheses

Poor:
Hypothesis 1. Older adults will be less able to ignore the interspersed irrelevant material than younger adults.
(Don't number the hypotheses like this. The dependent measure is not clear.)

Better:
It was anticipated that older adults would be less able to ignore the interspersed irrelevant material and, as a result, would read more slowly and show poorer comprehension than younger adults. (Adapted from Connelly, Hasher & Zacks, 1991, p. 534)

Poor:
Young men wanting to show off will take more risks when with other young men than in private.
('Wanting to show off' is too vague as an independent variable. How is it measured? Is there a control group? It should be written in the past tense.)

Better:
[The hypothesis was that] young men who wish to assert themselves and to gain prestige would tend to take greater risks in public when together with other young men, than would young men who do not have these wishes, whereas there would be no such difference in risk-taking in private. (Adapted from Dahlback, 1990, p. 532)
(In your Method section you should make clear how you measured 'wishing to assert themselves' and 'gaining prestige'.)

Poor:
The hypothesis is that student willingness to take a psychology course will depend on the gender of the instructor and the type of course being taught.
(It is not clear what is actually being measured. The prediction is too general. The tense is wrong.)

Better:
'[It was] hypothesised that student willingness to take a psychology course from a feminine, masculine or androgynous instructor would vary with the type of course being taught. Feminine and androgynous instructors would be preferred for clinical courses, which tend to emphasise personal/social skills. Masculine and androgynous instructors would be preferred for experimental courses, which tend to emphasise analytic/objective skills.' (Freeman, 1992, p. 93)

---

have chosen or been assigned, so you should be well aware of what was done. However, in the early undergraduate years, different tutorial groups are often given different treatments, or are presented with material in a different order from other groups. Your tutor or lecturer should make this clear, so don't rely solely on what you experienced in your group.

There are three reasons for having a Method section. One is to allow your reader to judge if your results are applicable to any other groups in which the reader is interested. The second is to allow someone else to repeat your study if they so desire, and to test your hypotheses on their particular sample. You therefore need sufficient detail so that someone else would be confident that by following your instructions they would be carrying out an identical experiment. The third reason is to allow a reader to judge whether your study really does test the hypotheses you claim that it tests.

The Method section is presented immediately after the Introduction without starting a new page. It is simply headed 'Method', in upper case and lower case lettering centred across the page. It contains a maximum of four subheadings:

- Participants (or Subjects, if non-human)
- Design
- Materials (or Apparatus)
- Procedure

Levels of headings The Method section is a good illustration of the necessity to distinguish between levels of headings. In most undergraduate lab reports there are only two levels of headings. One is the section headings, such as Method and Results, which have a capital letter, then lower case letters, and are centred across the page. The other is the subsection headings, which again have a capital, then lower case letters, but are aligned with the left margin, are italicised, and do *not* have a full stop. These conventions were introduced to make life easier for typesetters. Although you might argue that this reason doesn't apply to undergraduate lab reports, treat it as part of the discipline of writing to a convention. Once you know about it, you don't have to make decisions each time you write a lab report.

In later year lab reports, you may find that you need a third level of headings, for example, for different measures under the sub-heading of Materials. You should make these sub-sub-headings indented five spaces, italicised (or underlined), followed by a full stop. The content can then begin on the same line.

4.3.1 Participants

It should be noted that recent journals use the term 'participants' rather than 'subjects'. This reflects the current view that these people are not passive victims of you, the experimenter, but active partners in the research. Remembering how you may have felt while completing a questionnaire, or taking part in an experiment may remind you that not only are participants active, but their attitude to the study may not be what the experimenter really wanted. This should help you not to assume that they have done what you thought they were doing, and so you should regard the results with a critical and sceptical eye. 'Participant' is also more specific. For this reason, you should say 'children', 'clients', or 'patients' where they are applicable.

You should state the number of participants tested; how they were selected; refusal rates (if known); how they were rewarded; and any relevant demographic variables such as age, sex, education, ethnicity, occupational status, or other features. What makes a demographic variable relevant is if it is used as an independent variable (such as when comparing groups of different ages), or when it specifically defines the population from which the sample is drawn. Your statement of these details allows the reader to assess how adequately you have controlled for some of these variables, and the extent to which your findings can be generalised to any other groups. Examples are shown in Table 11.

Table 11

Examples of Descriptions of Participants in a Psychology Experiment

The participants were 130 female (M = 19.6 years, SD = 2.9 years) and 46 male (M = 19.7 years, SD = 2.9 years) undergraduate introductory psychology students of a Perth university who were participating as part of a course requirement.

The respondents were 97 women (M = 38.5 years, SD = 9.4 years), each chosen non-randomly by an introductory psychology student at a Sydney university. All subjects were or had been married, and had a mean education level of 11.4 years.

The sample comprised 78 children, 44 girls and 34 boys, attending Year 6 classes in two Brisbane suburban State schools serving predominantly middle-class populations.

The participants were 12 students from the Australian National University, who received $10 in return for their participation. All subjects had normal or corrected-to-normal vision and were native English speakers. (This was for an experiment on visual perception where vision is a relevant variable.)

Note

Note: You can say 'The sample was comprised of . . .' or 'The sample comprised . . .' or 'The sample consisted of . . .', but it is poor English to say 'The sample comprised of . . .' or 'The sample consisted 36 people . . .'. Similarly, don't say the 'The participants were divided into two groups . . .' because it gives the impression that each person was divided! Say 'The sample was divided into two groups . . .'.

4.3.2 Design

Check with your tutor or lecturer to find out if this subsection is required in your particular lab report. In many institutions it is not a required element of the Method section. However, it is sometimes expected in your first few undergraduate lab reports in order to show that you understand which are the independent and dependent variables. The purpose of the Design subsection is to lay out the basic conditions of the experiment and define dependent and independent variables. If you *are* required to include a Design subsection, state the independent and dependent variables in their operationalised form – that is, in the units in which they are measured – and describe the groups that are being compared, and any counterbalancing of the order in which material is presented.

When you are not expected to include a Design subsection, the operationalisation of the dependent and independent variables should be made clear in the Materials subsection where you describe how they are measured. If your study counterbalances the order of presentation of questionnaire items, say so in Materials. If different groups of participants are expected to perform different tasks, or to do them in different orders, describe this in the Procedure subsection.

4.3.3 Materials

If you use equipment, it must be described in sufficient detail so that anyone wishing to replicate the study can buy, build or otherwise acquire identical equipment. If you use a computer program, give its name, version number and source. If the layout of the equipment is either complex or theoretically important, for example, for some perception experiments, it may be necessary to include a diagram of the layout. In this case, you should label the section 'Apparatus' instead of 'Materials'. It may even make communication clearer if 'Apparatus' and 'Procedure' are combined into 'Apparatus and Procedure.' This allows you to say how the apparatus was used at the same time as you describe it.

In undergraduate studies, questionnaires are frequently used as the materials. If they are well-known psychological tests, include the author, date of publication, number of items and, if there are subscales within the test, state how many items are in each subscale. Also state briefly what you know of the test's psychometric properties, such as validity and reliability. State how the test was scored. If the questionnaire is one that was developed or adapted for your study, give a brief overview of it, include examples of an item or two, say how it was scored, and state that a copy is included as an Appendix. Several examples are included in Table 12. As long as you state in your report that such an Appendix exists, showing that you know what is expected, you need not actually have one there. Think of the trees and don't waste photocopy paper (or your money!). I will say a bit more about this in section 4.7 (Appendices).

If several scales are used in a questionnaire, it is not unusual to counterbalance the

Table 12

Examples of Overviews of Scales in a Materials Section

> Field-independence was measured by the Hidden Figures Test (HFT) (French et al., 1969). The 32-item HFT is a moderately difficult test requiring the ability to recognise simple geometric forms embedded within complex stimuli. Kardash et al. (1988) found that undergraduate students in educational psychology needed a score of 12 or better to be in the upper one-third of scores (field-independent), and a score of 8 or less to be in the lower one-third of scores (field-dependent). (Adapted from Townsend, Moore, Tuck & Wilton, 1990)
>
> Participants completed the Quality of Relationships Inventory (QRI) developed by Pierce et al. (1991). The QRI has three scales, two of which were of interest in the present study. These were: (a) expectations for Social Support (e.g. 'To what extent can you turn to this person for advice about problems?') and (b) Conflict (e.g. 'How often do you have to work hard to avoid conflict in this relationship?' and 'How much does this person make you feel guilty?'). (Adapted from Pierce, Sarason & Sarason, 1992)
>
> Rosenberg's (1965) 8-item Self-Esteem Scale (RSE) was used to assess self-esteem. Participants rated each item on a 5-point scale, where 1 = 'strongly disagree' and 5 = 'strongly agree'. Overall self-esteem scores were calculated by summing across all items after reversing some items for consistency of direction of expression. Note that lower scores indicate higher self-esteem.
>
> The three attachment vignettes originally created by Hazan and Shaver (1987) were decomposed into 13 individual sentences, each of which was answered on a 7-point Likert-type scale (1 = 'strongly disagree' and 7 = 'strongly agree'). To control for acquiescence response, five sentences were worded in a negative direction. An example is, 'I'm nervous whenever anyone gets too close to me. (Adapted from Simpson, Rholes & Nelligan, 1992)

order in which they are presented. That is, some participants will complete the scales in a particular sequence, while other participants will complete them in a different sequence. This allows the researcher to take account of possible practice, or learning effects. Typically, you should report it here in the Materials section. Having described the scales, say something like 'The order of presentation of the scales was counterbalanced to check for learning effects.'

Do *not* include materials that can be taken for granted, such as the fact that a pencil was used to fill in the questionnaire, or the location of the desk used, unless these are somehow pertinent to the results.

4.3.4 Procedure

This subsection is a fairly detailed description of how the study was carried out. Again, the detail should be such that it could confidently be replicated. For example, instructions given to participants should be quoted in full if they are fairly brief, or overviewed and referred to as present in an Appendix. Avoid abbreviations if you can. If you think abbreviations *are* necessary, use obvious ones that do not need tricky interpretations, and always define them the first time you use them. There are some examples illustrated in Table 13. Include how you controlled for extraneous nuisance factors, such as time, place and experimenter bias.

You should also describe how tests were administered and by whom. If deception is involved, include any 'cover story' you told the subjects. It is probably best to go through the procedure in the sequence that a subject experienced it, including debriefing, statements about written consent, whether you caused subjects to feel any embarrassment or discomfort, and whatever procedures you took to ensure anonymity. Kidder and Judd (1986) put it nicely when they say that you should describe how you ensured participants were treated with dignity and left with their self-esteem intact, and any respect they might have had for you and psychology enhanced rather than diminished.

Do *not* state that your tutor or lecturer collated the results for you, even though it may be true. Remember that you are writing the report as if *you* were the researcher who designed and carried out the study.

It is important not to confuse the Materials and the Procedure subsections. The Materials subsection describes what equipment or questionnaires were used in the study, and the Procedure subsection describes how the data were collected. Many modern journal articles do combine Materials and Procedure sections, but that is

Table 13

Examples of the Introduction of Abbreviations ✓

The sample comprised 46 monozygotic (MZ) and 52 dizygotic (DZ) twin pairs.

An analysis of variance (ANOVA) was calculated . . .

We propose an Abridged Big Five Dimensional Circumplex (AB5C) . . .

Participants completed the Minnesota Multiphasic Personality Inventory (MMPI).

Electromyographic (EMG) signals were measured with an eight-channel telemetry system . . .

usually because they are reporting multiple studies in one article. At undergraduate level, it is better to stick to the separate sections. When you get to the stage of writing for publication you can decide whether to 'bend the rules'.

4.4 Results

This section follows immediately after the Method section, and should *not* begin on a new page. The heading is simply 'Results', in upper case and lower case letters, and is centred.

The purpose of the Results section is to present in one place all the evidence relevant to your hypotheses. You should report your results in the same order that you used to present the hypotheses you made in the Introduction.

4.4.1 Your very first report

If this is your very first Results section, ask yourself: 'What information do I need to report to convince the reader that I really have tested the hypotheses?' Usually your first report will require few, if any, statistics. Typically, you are required to report frequency counts, or proportions. For example, you might have compared the proportion of drivers who fail to stop at a stop sign and who are male, with the proportion of drivers failing to stop at the same stop sign who are female. In this case you simply report that, for example, 'Of 100 drivers observed, 60 were male, and 11 of these failed to stop at the stop sign. Of the 40 female drivers, three failed to stop at the stop sign.' That allows your reader to make judgments of whether the sample size is reasonable, and to have the information to decide for themselves if your hypothesis was supported or not. If you are reporting the proportions of more than two groups, it may be simpler to show them as a bar chart. One example is shown in Figure 1, and the conventions for figures are described in section 4.4.6.

Some early lab reports expect you to calculate the mean and standard deviation of scores for two groups. For example, a classic study is one in which participants may have been asked to learn a list of pairs of words, where one group was given no explicit instructions, and the other was given instructions to imagine bizarre connections between the word pairs. They may then have been given one word from each pair in the list and expected to remember its pair. If your hypothesis was that the bizarre instructions should lead to better recall of the paired words, then reporting the mean number of words recalled correctly in each group will allow you to judge whether the instructions made a difference. A good way to report these results is: 'The bizarre imagery instructions resulted in more word pairs being correctly recalled (M = 13.2, SD = 4.3) than did the non-explicit instructions (M = 8.6, SD = 5.1).' The conventions for reporting statistics are described at page 61, but the M is the convention for the arithmetical mean, and the SD for standard deviation.

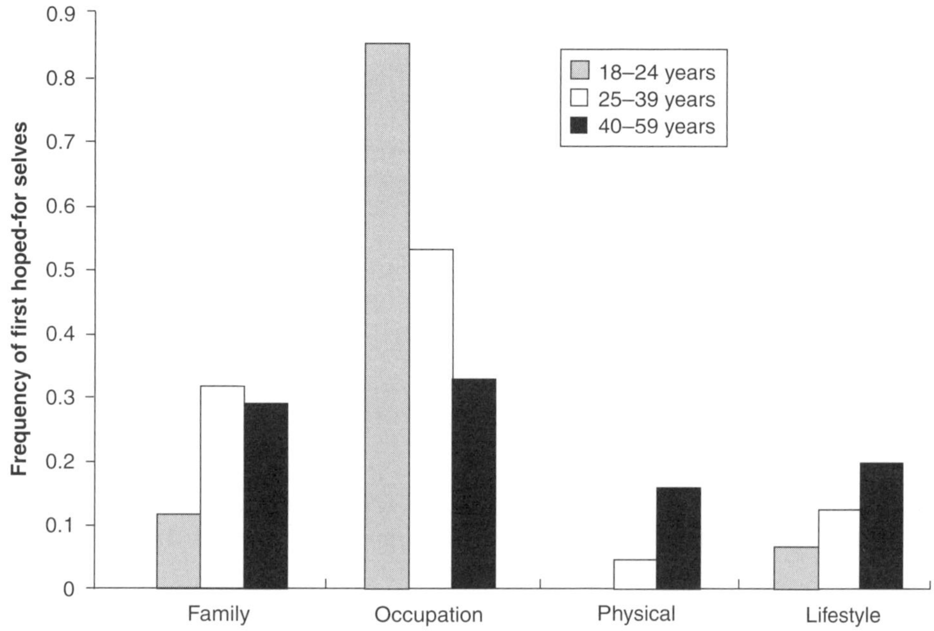

Figure 1. Differences in frequencies of first hoped-for selves across age groups. (From a lab report adapted from Cross and Markus, 1991)

I would strongly discourage the use of graphs or tables for reporting only one or two statistics. It is essential that you be able to construct grammatically correct sentences to say what you have found, and to insert the appropriate statistics into them. In reports where the statistics are numerous, and reporting them in sentence form is tedious and repetitive to read, then tables or graphs are appropriate, but even so, you need plain English statements to summarise the statistics and introduce the table. Students will lose marks for having a table unless it is properly introduced.

4.4.2 All reports

In lab reports in which statistics are calculated, especially if calculated using a computer package, it is advisable to begin the section with a statement about how the raw data were processed to produce the summary data. However, you should *not* have the raw data themselves in this section. Again, you should *not* say that your department or tutor or lecturer collated and summarised the data. Pretend that the data were manipulated by you in such a way that you could make inferences about the variables you have measured. If there were no effects due to counterbalancing, state this at the start of the Results section. There are some examples of introductory statements about data in Table 14.

You should introduce and present descriptive statistics first, usually means and standard deviations, or perhaps medians and semi-interquartile ranges. Then you should describe any inferential tests of significance that you have calculated, such as t-tests or analyses of variance (ANOVAs), and any post hoc comparisons of means.

Table 14

Examples of Introductory Statements in the Results Section

Results were analysed using the SPSS for Windows statistical package, version 11.5.

T-tests were calculated to compare mean scores for the groups of interest.

'First, to examine whether male and female partners differed overall on their scores on the three attachment dimensions, we compared the mean scores for men and women.' (Collins & Read, 1990, p. 657)

'Of 530 respondents at Time 1, three (0.6%) were excluded from analyses because they had missing data on 10 or more items of the NEO-FFI. Item level analyses were therefore performed on a sample of 527 participants.' (Murray, Rawlings, Allen & Trinder, 2003, pp. 131–140)

'The responses to the four initial on-line judgements were averaged to form an index, as were the four later memory-based judgements. Means are displayed in Table 4.' (Schul & Burnstein, 1990, p. 969)

All sets of items were analysed by a 3 (between subjects) × 2 (within subjects) analysis of variance (ANOVA). Scheffe tests were used for mean comparisons where appropriate.

Individual-participant mean latency data, collapsed over the eight trial blocks, were submitted to a repeated measures analysis of variance (ANOVA) to assess the effects that were due to judgment-type and stimulus complexity.

You should *not* assume that your reader has remembered everything already said. It is important to express your results in a way that makes clear that your hypotheses are being appropriately tested. You need to express yourself clearly so the reader is reminded of why the data are important and why they are being compared, but do your best not to be too repetitive. For studies where there are only one or two hypotheses, it is sufficient to simply report what you found, as shown in the previous section. For reports with more than two hypotheses, you might remind the reader what the hypothesis was by saying something like:

'A one-tailed paired-samples t-test found that respondents reported the quality of their own relationship to be significantly higher (M = 4.40, SD = .81) than that of the average person (M = 3.67, SD = .68), $t(120) = 8.58$, $p < .001$.'

If there were six paired comparisons made, you might put the means, standard deviations and t-statistics (t, degrees of freedom, and p) into a table. In such a case, having introduced the table by saying something like: 'Means, standard deviations, and t-statistics for all pairs of judgments are shown in Table 1', you could simply say, after the table, that 'As can be seen in Table 1, on average, respondents reported that their own relationships were significantly better than those of the average typical person.'

Reporting statistics There are strict conventions regarding how statistics are reported. Any ordinary letter representing a statistic should be italicised, and you should state the nature of the test, the degrees of freedom, the value of the statistic and the level of significance, in that order. Greek letters, such as Chi-square (χ^2) are *not* italicised. There are several examples of the conventions for reporting frequently used inferential statistics in Table 15.

Table 15

Examples of the Conventions of Reporting Statistical Findings

'A one-tailed t-test for independent samples indicated that the younger group had a significantly faster reaction time (M = 320 ms, SD = 48 ms) than the older group (M = 392 ms, SD = 56 ms), $t(38) = 4.37$, $p < .05$.

With lower levels of marital satisfaction, husbands tended to exhibit more avoidant behaviours, $r = -.28$, $p < .05$. Although the corresponding correlation for wives was in the expected direction, their marital satisfaction was unrelated to their avoidant behaviour, $r = -.07$, $p > .05$.

As shown in Table 3, intellectually disabled individuals were more than twice as likely as non-disabled adults to be the victims of a personal offence, $\chi^2(1, N = 300) = 32.22$, $p < .001$.

An analysis of variance (ANOVA) was performed on participants' rated satisfaction with their group's performance. This ANOVA revealed a significant main effect of own group feedback, $F(1,52) = 120.35$, $p < .001$. The main effect of other group feedback was not significant, $F(1,52) = 1.49$, $p > .05$, nor was the interaction between own group and other group feedback, $F(1,52) = 2.03$, $p > .05$.'

Note

Note: Roman letters indicating statistics are italicised, and the general information to be stated is: (a) the type of statistic, (b) degrees of freedom, (c) the calculated statistic itself, and (d) the significance level.

Significance levels There is some controversy among psychologists about how significance levels should be reported. Some argue that it is good science to set your significance level before you do the test, then just say whether that level was exceeded or not. Others argue that information is lost by following this strategy, and that if the test is highly significant, this should be shown. If your lecturer or tutor does not give specific guidelines on reporting the significance of a statistical test, the safest thing to do with significant results is to use whichever of .05, .01 or .001 is the smallest. Unless you have a good reason for being stricter, report non-significant results as having a significance level greater than .05. Examples of both significant and non-significant results of statistical tests are also shown in Table 15.

Stating whether hypotheses are supported There is no formal convention for when you should state whether a hypothesis is supported or not. If you only have one or two straightforward hypotheses, which are simply tested, it is best to leave such a statement until the start of the Discussion. In a more complex study it is usually acceptable to make a statement of support (or otherwise) in the Results section. You can do this succinctly by beginning your statements: 'As predicted . . .', or ending them with '. . . as hypothesised'. In a study where you report the results of, say, an analysis of variance, you would normally have the means and standard deviations in a table. Always report the interaction effect first. If it is not significant, then report the main effects, something like this:

'There was a significant main effect of type of relationship, F (1,180) = 15.31, $p < .001$. As shown in Table 1, own relationships were reported to be better than others' relations, as predicted.'

Remember that if the interaction effect *is* significant, it is often meaningless to discuss the main effects. Assuming that you hypothesised such an interaction, you could remind the reader of it, as follows:

'A significant interaction was found, F (2,203) = 10.64, $p < .001$. An inspection of the means in Table 1 indicated, as hypothesised, that the difference reported between own and others' relationships was greater for romantic relationships than for parental ones.'

Note that in more advanced lab reports you may have been expected to perform post hoc tests to determine this, not a simple inspection of the means. However, do not make any further interpretation of the results beyond the simple statement of support, as illustrated. Check with your tutor or lecturer about their preference.

4.4.3 Numbers and words

When reading journal articles you will sometimes see numbers written in words (three, eight), and sometimes as Arabic numerals (11, 124). The convention is that you should use numerals to express numbers 10 and above (e.g., 'the remaining 10 participants', '25 years old') and words for the numbers one to nine. The exception is where numbers below 10 are grouped for comparison with a number of 10 or above (e.g. '3 of 21 analyses'). You should also use numerals when they precede a unit of measurement (e.g., '2 cm', '5 mg dose').

Use words to express any number at the beginning of a sentence (e.g., 'Seventy-four children participated . . .'), or numbers below 10 that do not fit the previously mentioned criteria ('a total of six items . . .'), or common fractions ('one-fifth of the class . . .', 'reduced by two-thirds . . .'). Use a combination of figures and words to express rounded large numbers ('almost 3 million people . . .') and back-to-back modifiers ('two 2-way interactions', 'eight 6-year-olds').

4.4.4 Decimals

The number of decimal places reported should reflect the precision of your measurement. If the number is the mean of an array of integers, use only one decimal place. Two decimal places are usually the most you will need in undergraduate reports. Do *not* use more than two decimal places, even if your computer printout does! It gives a false impression of the accuracy of your measurement. The convention is to round up the second decimal place if the third digit is 5 or greater, and to round down if it is 4 or less. For example, 4.235 should round to 4.24, but 4.234 should round to 4.23.

Use a zero before the decimal point when numbers are less than one, except where the number, by its nature, cannot be greater than one, such as correlations, proportions, and levels of statistical significance. For example use '0.23cm' but '$r = .74$, $p < .05$.'

4.4.5 Tables

One of the most frequent errors that students make in presenting results is to assume that a table or figure is sufficient, or even essential. *This is not true*. Tables or figures should be regarded as optional extras, to be used only to summarise complex results, which are repetitive to read. They should *not* replace the text. Never draw up a table for a single t-test result or a single correlation. Such results are best reported by a standard sentence.

There is a good deal of evidence indicating that even experts are poor at interpreting many tables and figures without good instructions. You should therefore tell the reader what to look for in your table or figure and give enough explanation to make the table or figure easily understandable, before the table or figure appears in your report. Some examples of introductions to tables and figures are shown in Table 16.

In your early lab reports, tables and figures are shown as soon as possible after you introduce them. That will usually be before the next paragraph starts, with a couple of spaces before and after them to set them off from your text. However, it is important that tables or figures and their titles are not split over two pages, so it is acceptable to separate them from when you introduced them by another paragraph. Leave a couple of spaces after a table or figure before you start the next paragraph.

Table 16

Introductions to Tables and Figures

Figure 1 displays the mean number of correctly recalled nonsense syllables and the mean number of correctly recalled meaningful words on each of the first 10 trials.

Table 5 shows the proportions of participants who responded in each category in each condition.

Table 4 presents the correlations between the two sub-scales of the Marital Satisfaction Scale and the three sub-scales of the Eating Attitudes Scale.

The participant's payoffs for the two choices as a function of the number of others who invest in the joint account are shown in Table 1.

The model, presented in Figure 2, shows that there is very little relationship among feedback, attention to inconsistency, and impressions.

Mean liking ratings can be seen in Figure 4.

There are conventions for the presentation of tables and figures that you must adhere to. Tables are numbered successively, using Arabic integers only (1, 2, 3 . . .). Each has a title at the top, which should be clear and explanatory, preferably stating the relationship between the independent and dependent variables shown in the table. The table number should be on a line of its own, not underlined or in italics. The title should begin on the next line and should be italicised. You should capitalise the first letter of all major words in the title. There are some examples of good titles for both tables and figures in Table 17.

When preparing an article for publication, tables are expected to be double-spaced. This is less critical in an undergraduate report, but avoid small, cramped tables. Separate sections of a table with horizontal lines, but *never* include vertical lines in your tables (so avoid the temptation to show off your computer's grid-drawing capabilities!). If your table contains comparisons between groups, include the sample sizes of the groups. Use a note below the final horizontal line to explain anything that might not be immediately obvious, such as abbreviations, but unless impossible due to length, use the full names of variables, not their abbreviations or the names used by the computer as variable names. An example of a typical simple table is shown in Table 18, and a more complex one in Table 19. A table of correlations is shown in Table 20.

Tables usually present quantitative data. In undergraduate reports they will almost invariably be collections of numbers, appropriately identified. However, a table could

Table 17

Examples of Titles of Tables and Figures

Table 3
Mean Reaction Times of Younger and Older Participants

Table 1
Mean Anagram Solution Times for Three Groups of Differing Task Complexity

Table 2
Correlations Among Components of Defensiveness Composite Score and Independent Variables

Figure 1. Mean number of correctly recalled nonsense syllables and meaningful words over ten trials.

Figure 3. Means of marital satisfaction by age and stage of family life cycle.

Note which sections are italicised, and which words require the first letter to be capitalised.

Table 18

Mean Anagram Solution Times for Three Groups of Differing Task Complexity

Task	*n*	Mean time (in seconds)
Difficult	12	51.6
Moderate	13	43.8
Easy	9	29.2
N = 34		

Note: For any report except perhaps the very first one you do, you would need standard deviations as well.

Table 19

Mean Responses of High and Low Conservative Subjects to Individual and Corporate Wrongdoing

	Conservatism	
	High	Low
Judgment of Wrongdoing Items	*M*	*M*
Individual		
Knew beforehand	1.33	1.44
Recklessness	2.33	2.11
Morally wrong	2.56	2.11
Deserves punishment	2.22	2.22
Harm to workers	2.89	3.56
Fairness of criminal charge	2.67	1.89
Corporation		
Knew beforehand	2.09	2.00
Recklessness	3.18	4.09
Morally wrong	3.18	3.73
Deserves punishment	3.46	3.55
Harm to workers	3.46	3.46
Fairness of criminal charge	3.37	3.46

$N = 40$

Note: In more advanced reports, you would be expected to include standard deviations in brackets beside each value, and perhaps a t statistic and significance level if you used one to compare the high and low conservative means for each category.

Table 20

Intercorrelations Between Lemon Sourness and Personality Variables

	1	2	3	4	5
1. Sourness	*	$-.34^{\dagger}$	.09	.08	$.25^{\dagger}$
2. Extraversion		*	$-.16^{\dagger}$	−.08	−.10
3. Neuroticism			*	$.56^{\dagger}$	$.17^{\dagger}$
4. Arousability (SEA)				*	$.17^{\dagger}$
5. Arousal					*

$N = 324$, † = significant at $p < .05$
SEA = Scale of Emotional Arousability (Braithwaite, 1987)

Note: In a more advanced report, you could put the Cronbach alpha reliabilities for the appropriate subscales on the diagonal instead of asterisks.

include any other material which may be typeset, such as the examples in this book. Anything else is called a figure.

4.4.6 Figures

In an undergraduate laboratory report a figure will usually be a graph or a histogram, or occasionally a diagram of apparatus. In journal articles figures could include photographs or drawings.

Figures are also numbered sequentially in Arabic numerals. The title of a figure should go below the figure. The figure number should be italicised, but the title itself should not be underlined. Furthermore, the only capital letter should be the first letter of the first word of the title. Look at Table 17 again for some examples of figure titles.

In undergraduate laboratory reports the figure should not be smaller than about 8 cm × 12 cm, nor larger than about half a page. Leave a clear space of at least 2 cm above and below the figure so that it stands clear of the text. *Never* continue text alongside a figure. *Never* extend a figure over two pages, or split the figure and its title over two pages.

The height of the figure should be about two-thirds its width. Each axis of a graph or histogram should be clearly labelled. It is conventional to plot the independent variable on the horizontal axis and the dependent variable on the vertical axis. Break the axis with a double slash if the origin of the co-ordinates is not zero. Remember to mark accurately the plotted points on a graph. Figure 2 is a typical figure from an undergraduate report.

When producing figures you should ensure that they convey the message you intend.

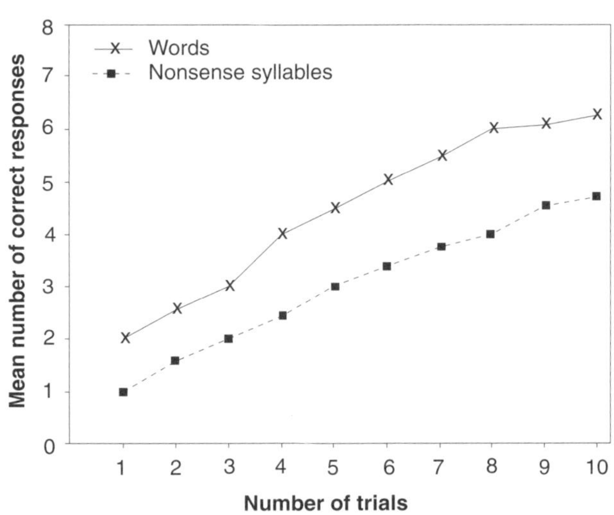

Figure 2. Mean number of correctly recalled nonsense syllables and meaningful words over 10 trials.

If a result is statistically significant, ensure that the figure shows the difference. A statistically non-significant result should also be reflected in your figure. This is largely a matter of choosing the appropriate scales for your axes. The importance of this is shown by comparing Figure 3 and Figure 4. If the results being reported are non-significant, then a figure is not necessary. You could just say so in words. If the results *are* significant, Figure 3 does not give any idea about how different they are, where Figure 4 does show the difference. Note however, that if the differences were not significant, and you showed them in Figure 4, then a false impression of difference

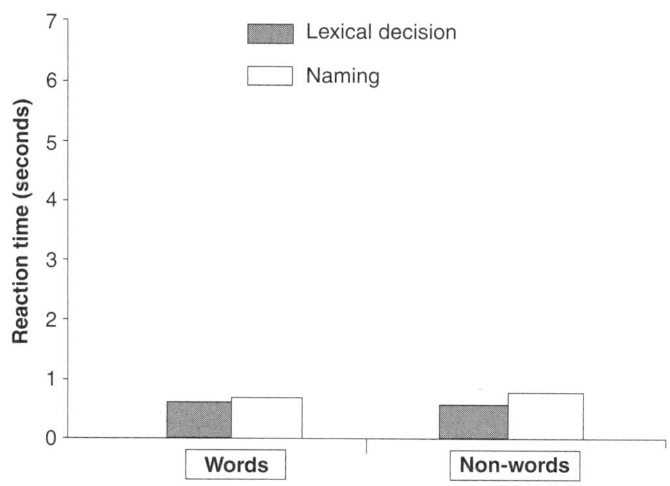

Figure 3. The data shown in this Figure are the same as in Figure 4, but are given in seconds, so any differences are minimised.

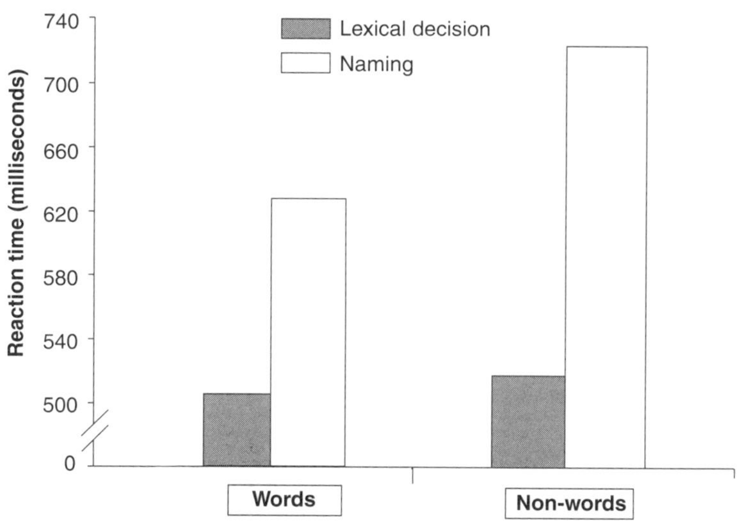

Figure 4. The data shown in this figure are the same as in Figure 3, but are shown here in milliseconds so that differences are accentuated.

is given. What makes it false is the slashes showing that the vertical axis does not show the whole number, but only a small part of it.

If figures of two sets of results are to be compared, make sure that they have exactly the same axes, otherwise your readers will have to make complicated transformations in their heads, which will hinder your message and lose you marks.

4.5 Discussion

The Discussion, as in the Method and Results sections, follows straight on with the single word 'Discussion' in upper case and lower case letters centred on the page. It is *not* necessary to start a new page.

Remember that in the first chapter the report was described as being like an hourglass in shape. The Discussion can be viewed as the other end of the hourglass from the Introduction. Where the Introduction begins with a broad statement of the area under study and becomes more specific as you argue the case for your particular hypotheses, the Discussion should begin specifically and then broaden out. The Discussion begins with specific statements about whether the hypotheses were supported. These statements are followed by interpretation of the results, and discussion of how your results relate to the studies you mentioned in the Introduction. At the end of the Discussion, the hourglass is again at its broadest with discussion of the implications your results have for the 'real world', although you should avoid such a flippant expression! Let's look at each of these parts of the Discussion in more detail.

State whether hypotheses have been supported You should not expect your reader to remember exactly what your hypotheses were, so it is advisable to restate them. However, avoid repeating information already in the Results section. For example, you could say, 'The results of the current study support the hypothesis that parents perceive greater similarity between their children than those children perceive between themselves.'

Be very careful about what your results tell you. *Never* use the words 'prove' or 'disprove'. A single experiment does not unequivocally disprove a hypothesis, and no hypothesis can ever be proved. Someone could always come along and think of a different explanation, which also fits the observed facts. What you should say is that your results support, or fail to support, your hypotheses.

If you have several hypotheses, it is best to begin your Discussion with a paragraph in which you state whether each of the hypotheses is supported or not, and how you know. In the following paragraphs you should then discuss each one to completion before interpreting the next. Discussing each hypothesis in turn gives your Discussion greater coherence and continuity. The danger is in repeating your hypotheses frequently, which gets boringly repetitive. It is acceptable to have an introductory sentence stating that 'Results indicate that all (or most of) the hypotheses were supported.' Or, 'While the hypothesis that . . . was supported by the results, there was only partial support for the prediction that . . .'. The following paragraphs could elaborate on the details, and whether your results support previous findings.

Interpretation of results – support for previous research The interpretation of results relating to any one hypothesis should be dealt with in two ways. The first way is to relate your results to previous research. Make a brief but clear statement of whether the results are or are not compatible with the research you described in your Introduction, and which led to you making that particular hypothesis. For example, 'The observation that the groups asked to rate whether words were pleasant or unpleasant had better recall than those asked to judge whether the words contained the letter "e" is consistent with the findings of Hyde and Jenkins (1969).' This is the second time in the Discussion that the hypothesis has been stated, although perhaps in a slightly different form. That should be enough. Constant repetition of the hypothesis is irritating to a reader. You need to find a balance between reminding the reader what the hypothesis is, and boring them to death with it. Note that your results support (or confirm) previous research. Theirs came first, so it is not accurate to say that their work supports your findings!

Interpretation of results – explanation of findings The second way that your results need to be dealt with is at the level of explanation. In the first few lab reports you will encounter, the chances are that you will be replicating a previously published study. Replication is one of the aspects of the scientific method, and its importance should not be underestimated. You will therefore know how the author or authors of that study interpreted their results. In that case you can put their explanation into your own words. Following the sentence in the previous example you could say, 'Hyde and Jenkins interpreted such findings as supporting the depth of processing theory, that material processed at the semantic or deep level would be better remembered than material processed at the surface level of appearance.' Remember that since you have just referred to Hyde and Jenkins (1969) in the previous sentence, you do not have to repeat the year of publication. However, if it were a new paragraph, you *would* be expected to include the year of publication.

If your study is not a replication of a previous study, then you have to be more thoughtful in finding a possible explanation for the results you obtained. There are two major types of explanation possible for a particular set of results. One explanation is based on theoretical considerations and the other on methodological considerations. The distinction is illustrated by the following example from Macrae (1989).

Suppose a psychologist, Jane Bloggs, theorises that, due to a genetic factor, males are superior to females in spatial ability and she finds that several studies exist to support this theory. Suppose that you have just designed a new test of spatial ability and have administered it to a large number of psychology undergraduates. There are three possible outcomes, with two possible explanations for each.

The first possible outcome is that you find that males perform better on your test.

One explanation is that, based on the Bloggs theory, you hypothesised that males would do better; the results supported your hypothesis and, by inference, the theory is further supported. A different explanation is that your spatial test and most others are biased because the items tend to be selected from material that males are more likely to have encountered at school. Although there *is* a gender difference, it is not due to genetic factors but to differential socialisation of males and females.

The second possible outcome is that you find no difference between mean scores for males and females. One explanation is that since you had hypothesised that males would do better, based on the Bloggs theory, and your results do not support your hypothesis, then doubt is cast on previous findings and on the theory. However, another explanation would be that female university students are not representative of the general female population, but actually have higher spatial ability than most females, while male university students are more typical of the general population of males, at least in spatial ability. Your failure to find a gender difference actually reflects inadequate sampling from the population to which the Bloggs theory applies.

The third possibility is that females score better on spatial ability than males. As in the previous paragraph, your results do not support your hypothesis, and so doubt is cast on the Bloggs theory. Again, as in the previous paragraph, a different explanation is that female university students are better at spatial ability than most other females, while, in contrast to the previous paragraph, male university students are actually worse than most other males. Once again, your failure to support your hypothesis reflects inadequate sampling from the general population.

In each possible outcome, the first explanation is a straightforward theoretical one. Either the theory is supported or not. The second explanation for each outcome reinforces the importance of not being dogmatic about proving things. A different but quite logical explanation fits the same observed facts. In the second explanation for each outcome, there are methodological considerations affecting the results. These considerations are themselves capable of being tested in later research. A good lab report would recognise that there are alternative explanations and would recommend ways of testing them.

Methodological considerations You also need to deal with other possible methodological considerations in your Discussion section. Doing so indicates that you are aware of extraneous factors that may have affected your results. However, you need to distinguish between faults in design and problems in procedure. An example of a design fault is an investigation of the effectiveness of two different lecturers, which uses one class where the students are on average 10 years older than those in the other class. The effects of lecturer are confounded with the effects of age. It is unlikely that you will find such design flaws in a study designed by psychology staff.

An example of a procedural problem is running a well-designed study under crowded and noisy conditions. A common problem with students' reports is that they waste space in the Discussion in criticising the conduct of the experiment. Many undergraduate experiments run as teaching exercises are impossible to run under ideal conditions.

Since you should be writing the report as if it was a study that you had designed yourself, you should not do a hatchet job on the psychology department's running of the exercise under inadequate conditions. You should certainly discuss faulty design, specifically describing any systematic effects this may have had on the results. However, procedural problems such as varying ages, times of testing (day and evening students), crowded conditions, noise and similar factors *rarely* have systematic effects on the results. They should *not* be mentioned in your discussion unless you can convince your reader that they *did* have a systematic effect, which was reflected in the results, and which would have changed the conclusions you made. Unless the effect is clearly visible in the results, you cannot say that the problem has occurred. Simply saying that something 'may' have affected the results will lose you marks. If you want to let your reader know that you have thought about these factors, you should say something like: 'Although subject to the usual problems associated with undergraduate experiments (or studies, or procedures), no obvious systematic effects on the results were observed.'

Implications Having discussed the compatibility of your results with those of previous research, given an explanation for the results, and mentioned any design problems that may have become apparent, you need to discuss the implications of the results. The explanation you gave for the results you obtained will presumably be applicable more widely than for the specific instance you tested. Say how this might be so, especially if the results allow you to extend or consolidate a theory.

Usually, undergraduate studies have a fairly applied flavour, so you should be able to say what the implications of your results are for the wider community. Keep in mind, however, that there may be other explanations, so avoid being dogmatic. For example, in a questionnaire study of attitudes to corporate or individual responsibility for wrongdoing, you may find that people judge corporations more harshly. You could then state that such a finding has implications for how monetary compensation is calculated in legal settlements.

Conclusion Finally, you need a concluding paragraph that sums up what the study has found. It is sometimes easier to state what future research should be done to take your findings a step further, or to control for faulty design that became apparent in the running of the experiment. This should be done carefully. It is boring and glib simply to say that more research needs to be done. You must be specific in saying what variables need to be accounted for or controlled.

It is better to have a concluding paragraph that is a neat precis of the study, emphasising the conclusions you have reached. An example from a first-year report might look like this:

> In conclusion, this study has revealed that people perceive their future selves most often in terms of their occupational or career opportunities. This was particularly evident in the younger age groups. The area of family was also

> considered important. Relative levels of well-being seemed to generate no real difference in participants' perceptions of possible future selves. All participants, irrespective of age, felt capable of achieving their future selves.

The Discussion is the last section in the body of the report. As mentioned earlier, it is usually easiest to write the Method section first, then the Results, then the Introduction, and finally the Discussion. Having written a first draft of all these sections, you should give them, in the correct order, to someone else to read critically. Based on the feedback you receive from this person, you should redraft your report. Then repeat the process, getting someone else to read your second draft. Any student serious about achieving a pass should do at least this much: a rough draft, then a second one that will need only minor modifications before being typed.

Having had your second draft critically read, you are ready to add the finishing touches. The Abstract and Title Page have already been mentioned. You now need to deal with the Reference list and the Appendices.

4.6 References

This section comes after the Discussion, is written with a capital and then lower case letters, centred across the page, and *does* begin on a new page. It is important to recognise that this section is *not* a bibliography. A bibliography is a list of all the references that you have consulted, even if you have not included them in the final report. *Do not* include a bibliography in a psychology laboratory report.

You should put into your Reference list *all* those references, and *only* those references, that you have referred to in the body of your report, *and that you have actually read*. If you read in your textbook that James (1890) said something, it is the textbook that should be in the reference list, *not* James (1890). If your marker sees a particularly interesting or obscure reference, they might ask you for a copy of it. If you don't have it, you will be in trouble! Similarly, if you only read the abstract in *PsychInfo*, but not the entire article, be honest in your Reference list. So, remember that if you have written 'Stoner (1961, cited in Turner, Hogg & Wetherell, 1991)' then only the Turner, Hogg and Wetherell (1991) reference is included in the Reference list. Note that all types of references, journal articles, books and book chapters are all mixed in together in a single list. I've separated the categories in the section that follows, but only for your convenience in checking out the conventional format. You should include them all in the one list.

Most markers are fairly strict about adhering to the conventions for Reference lists of the *Publication Manual* of the APA. Many students are careless about this. Although it may appear pedantic to be concerned about punctuation, the conventions are easy to learn, and a good Reference list is a simple way to pick up a mark, leaving your marker with the impression that you care enough about your work to attend to detail.

Order of references The Reference list is in the alphabetical order of the surname of the first author of each work cited in the body of your report. If there are two authors of the same surname, it goes by alphabetical order of their first initial. If you cite two works by the same author, they go in chronological order of year of publication. If you cite two works by the same author published in the same year, call them, for example, (1999a) and (1999b) in both the body of the report and the Reference list. Articles by an author alone go before those by the same author with co-authors. Articles by an author with different co-authors go in alphabetical order of the second author's surname.

You must *not* change the order of authors in any one article. There is an academic pecking order which makes the order of authors important, since the assumption is that the first author usually has done the greater amount of work on the article. If you don't see why this is important, how do you refer to your text? Even if it has been written by several authors, the chance is that you refer to it by the name of the first author. If professional kudos are gained by being well known, being first author of a book is important!

Specific examples of the conventions for listing particular types of references that you are likely to come across are given below. If you wish to use some of the more exotic examples of references, see the *Publication Manual* of the APA for details.

Format and style of references The *Publication Manual* of the APA was written to tell authors the conventions of preparing a manuscript for publication, and is designed to make life easy for publishers of journals. That is one reason why some of the fussier conventions regarding lab reports have come into being. However, with the latest edition of the manual, common sense has prevailed with at least two areas that have given students some trouble in the past. One is the format of your reference list. The current expectation, which is the easiest to read, is that the first line of the reference is flush with the left margin, and the second and later lines are indented one tab, or about 1 cm.

The second improvement is that it is now expected that you will use italics rather than underlining, not only in references, but also in statistics. The purpose of underlining was to tell the typesetter what to put in italics in the published version. But since all word processing packages have an italics function it seems silly not to use it, and the latest edition of the APA *Manual* now recognises this.

4.6.1 Books

An entry in the Reference list should contain all the information necessary for identification and library search, including place and date of publication, publisher's name and the edition. The convention is to use italics for some parts of the references. Note also the location of commas and periods (full stops). The title has a capital letter only for the first letter of the first word. The first line is flush with the left margin, and all following lines within that reference are indented about 1 cm.

First editions

Abrams, A., & Hogg, M.A. (1999). *Social identity and social cognition*. Malden, MA, USA: Blackwell.

OR

Latta, R.L. (1998). *The basic humor process*. Berlin: Mouton de Gruyter.

If a new edition

Carlson, N.R., & Buskist, W. (1997). *Psychology: The science of behavior*. (5th ed.). Boston: Allyn and Bacon.

OR

Biddulph, S. (1995). *Manhood* (2nd ed.). Sydney: Finch Publishing.

An edited book

Skevington, S., & Baker, D. (Eds.). (1989). *The social identity of women*. London: Sage.

A specific chapter in an edited book

Moore, S. (1999). Sexuality in adolescence: A suitable case for coping. In E. Frydenberg (Ed.). *Learning to cope: Developing as a person in complex societies*, pp. 64–80. London: Oxford University Press.

4.6.2 Journal articles

Note that the title of the journal, and the volume number (but not the page numbers), are italicised and that capital letters for the beginning of major words are used only for the names of the journals. In some references you will read, you will see a number in brackets after the volume number. Don't do this. It is only for the case where the page numbers start again from 1 with every new issue of that journal, which is not the case for most modern psychology journals, where the page numbers are continuous over the whole year's issues.

Journal article, one author

Forgas, J.P. (1998). On being happy and mistaken: Mood effects on the fundamental attribution error. *Journal of Personality and Social Psychology, 75*, 318–331.

OR

Kressin, N.R. (1996). The effect of medical socialization on medical students' need for power. *Personality and Social Psychology Bulletin, 22*, 91–98.

Journal article, two authors

Faelli, R.C., & Carless, S.A. (1999). A comparison of psychological characteristics of employed and unemployed professionally qualified immigrants. *Australian Psychologist, 34*, 183–187.

OR

Knight, R.G., & Godfrey, P.D. (1996). Psychosocial aspects of neurological disorders: Implications for research in neuropsychology. *Australian Psychologist, 31*, 48–51.

Journal article, more than two authors

Anshel, M.H., Robertson, M., & Caputi, P. (1997). Sources of acute stress and their appraisals and reappraisals among Australian police as a function of previous experience. *Journal of Occupational and Organizational Psychology, 70*, 337–356.

Journal article accepted for publication, but not yet published This convention applies to articles that a publisher has accepted, but that have not yet actually been published.

Grossbaum, M.F., & Bates, G.W. (in press). Determinants of psychological well-being at midlife: The role of generativity, agency and communion, and narrative themes. *International Journal of Behavioral Development*.

Periodical published annually Treat annually published series, such as the *Annual Review of Psychology*, that have specified, regular publication dates as periodicals, not as books.

Bentler, P.M., & Dudgeon, P. (1996). Covariance structure analysis: Statistical practice, theory, and directions. *Annual Review of Psychology, 47*, 563–592.

Conference papers

Findlay, B.M., & Kaufmann, K. (2002, July). *Negative uses of humour: Teasing, sarcasm and irony*. Paper presented at the 14th conference of the International Society of Humour Studies. Bertinoro, Forli, Italy.

Abstract only

If you find an interesting abstract using *PsychInfo*, you need to be honest about admitting that you've only seen the abstract, not the entire article. Many such abstracts are doctoral dissertations. Here's how you stay honest:

Brewster, M.K. (2000). Entering and exiting the corporation: A developmental study of women executives at mid-life. *Dissertation Abstracts International: Section B: The Sciences & Engineering, Vol 60(9-B)*. pp. 4877.

4.6.3 Internet sources

Articles obtained from the Internet Most libraries subscribe to electronic databases of journals as well as keeping printed versions on campus. If you obtain a photocopy from your library, which the library has obtained from such a database, or you download it from the web, you need to acknowledge this.

Increasingly, material will become more easily available from the Internet than from hard copies in libraries. The latest edition of the *Publication Manual* of the APA includes conventions for referencing such material. The purpose of a reference is to enable someone else to obtain the same material you used, so it is important to give enough detail to allow that.

In Chapter 6 I expand on how you should use the Internet for lab reports and essays, but essentially I advise you to stick to electronic versions of journal articles. Here is how you should reference them.

Internet article based on a print source (i.e., there is also a printed version, but you've accessed it through your library's electronic service)

Heaven, P.C.L., & Goldstein, M. (2001). Parental influences and mental health among some Australian youth: Crosscultural analysis [Electronic version]. *Australian Journal of Psychology, 53,* 170–175.

Article in an Internet-only journal

Fricker, J., & Moore, S. (2002). Relationship satisfaction: The role of love styles and attachment styles. *Current Research in Social Psychology, 7.* Retrieved June 17, 2002 from http://www.uiowa.edu/~grpproc/crisp/crisp.html.

Both the above articles would be cited in the body of your text in the same way you would cite any journal article, that is, as Heaven and Goldstein (2001) and Fricker and Moore (2002) respectively.

Document created by a private individual or organisation

Harris, R. Virtual Salt: *Evaluating internet research sources.* Retrieved July 1, 2002 from http://www.virtualsalt.com/evalu8it.htm.

That article is well worth a look! If there is no obvious author, use any reasonable title from the site, like this:

ResearchBUZZ. *News and information about search engines and databases.* Retrieved August 11, 2002 from http://researchbuzz.com/index.shtml.

The APA *Manual* is not clear about citations in text of electronic sources, so the rule of thumb is to make it clear enough that the interested reader (your marker!) can find it in your reference list. For the above examples, I'd recommend using the author, if one is available, or the title if there is no clear author, and the retrieval date. For example, Harris (2002) and ResearchBUZZ (2002).

If you wish to reference a web site, but not a specific document within that site, you need only give the URL in the text, and **not** have it in the Reference list. For example, you might say:

An amusing site for aficionados of psychological tests is http://www.queendom.com. (omit the last full stop – I couldn't bring myself to omit one from the end of a sentence!)

4.6.4 Other sources

Entry in an encyclopedia

Bergman, P.G. (1993). Relativity. In *The new encyclopedia Britannica.* (Vol. 26, pp. 501–508). Chicago: Encyclopedia Britannica.

Unpublished thesis

These are often catalogued and available in the library from graduate students at your university, and are a good source of recent research.

Feeney, J.A. (1990). *The attachment perspective on adult romantic relationships.* Unpublished doctoral dissertation, University of Queensland, St Lucia.

Newspaper articles

You should **never** cite a newspaper article in a lab report, but you may use one in an essay or other piece of assessment.

Heath, S. (1995, August 24). Family life in the '90s: Finding the right mix. *The Age*, p. 4.

This would be cited in the body of your essay as Heath (1995), just like any journal article. If there was no author acknowledged, show it in the Reference list as follows, alphabetised by the first significant word in the title.

Family life in the '90s: Finding the right mix. (1995, August 24). *The Age*, p. 4.

In the body of your essay, you would cite this, in brackets, as (Family life, 1995).

Magazine article
Again, you should **never** include a magazine citation in a lab report, but the format is very similar to a newspaper article.

Rowe, D. (1999, November 27). Feeling glad all over. *Good Weekend*, pp. 43–45.

Please note carefully in each of the above examples which parts are italicised, which words are given upper case letters, and where there are punctuation marks.

4.7 Appendices

It is rare for a journal article to include any Appendices at all. However, it is not unusual for student lab reports to do so. In many psychology departments, students are requested to include their statistical analyses, either by hand or computer printouts. This is to allow the marker to check that what you state in the Results section has been correctly calculated. It also allows for realistic damage control. If you have made a mathematical error that affects your interpretation of the test of a hypothesis, then you will typically be penalised only for that one mistake, even though it affects the remainder of your report, as long as the remainder of the report is consistent with the mistaken interpretation.

Another occasion where the inclusion of statistical calculations is especially important is in cases where you have been expected to *create* one or more hypotheses to test rather than having them given to you. Your marker needs to know that the statistic quoted to test a hypothesis has been correctly applied and calculated.

Also, given the word limits usually imposed, there is often insufficient space to completely describe a questionnaire designed for the report. In that case, the place for the questionnaire is logically the Appendix. Sometimes it is impractical to include the actual questionnaire or test, or the materials used in an experiment, such as word lists. As long as you have said in your Materials section that an Appendix contains it, and have given an appropriate, if brief description including number of items, an example or two of items, and any psychometric properties known, then you have met the expected convention. Your marker does not have to actually see the questionnaire, so you may as well save photocopy time, money and paper. Check with your tutor or lecturer, but it will usually be acceptable to either omit the questionnaire from an Appendix, or include a single sheet saying that the appended material would normally be there. In the interests of saving paper, I favour omitting everything other than statistical calculations from the Appendix entirely.

You should *not* include tables or figures in an Appendix. If tables or figures relating to your results are worth drawing up, then they belong in the Results section.

Format of Appendices If there is only one Appendix, label it 'Appendix' with a capital then lower case, centred across the page. If there are more than one, call them Appendix A, Appendix B, etc followed by the title, centred across the page, for example:

Appendix A
List of anagrams and their solutions used in group size experiment

When you have got this far, you can breathe a sigh of relief. All you need to do is put the completed report in a folder with your name and class details on it and hand it in. If you have been efficient with your time management, you should still have 48 hours or so before the report is due. Do not forget to have the final typed copy proofread, and any typos corrected (white-out and handwritten corrections are acceptable). Also, remember to keep a copy of the final report, either a photocopy, or a file on a computer disk.

4.8 Further reading

The major arbiter of current convention in psychological report writing is the *Publication Manual* of the APA. Here is the full reference:

American Psychological Association. (2001). *Publication manual.* (5th ed.). Washington, DC: Author.

This book gives minute details of the conventions for writing articles intended to be published in APA journals. If you intend to become an academic psychologist, this book is an essential purchase. You can usually find a copy on counter reserve in your library, and I encourage you to have a look at it.

Another useful book is Sternberg's on writing scientific reports. Although it says it is for students, it is really aimed at researchers at the beginning of their research publication careers. However, it is quite readable, and if your library has a copy it is well worth having a look at it. Here is the reference:

Sternberg, R.J. (1993). *The psychologist's companion: A guide to scientific writing for students and researchers.* (3rd ed.). Cambridge: Cambridge University Press.

A book that is very useful on general study skills, including library skills, is one by Neil Burdess. It has excellent sections on general writing skills, essay writing, and preparing for lectures, tutorials, and exams.

Burdess, N. (1991). *The handbook of student skills for the social sciences and humanities.* Sydney: Prentice Hall Australia.

4.9 Feedback

As a marker, I feel very frustrated if I have written what I believe to be helpful comments on students' reports, and find students look only at the grade they receive then put the report away. It will help you if you read the marker's comments when you get your report back. Do not rush up to your tutor or lecturer demanding an immediate explanation. Some institutions have a policy that assignment grades will not be discussed for 24 hours after their return. Take the report home and think about what has been commented on, as it relates to what you wrote. If you are still unclear about what is meant, make an appointment to speak to your tutor or lecturer about the report at a mutually convenient time, if possible. Make notes about that discussion and keep them with the report. Next time you have to write a report, all the material will be together, and will save you having to start from the beginning again.

It is certainly distressing to have put in a lot of work and then find that it has not been rewarded with the grade you expected. However, in spite of what I said about lifting your marks with each redrafting, there is not necessarily a direct relationship between effort and grades. Psychology lab reports are different from most forms of assignment that you will be familiar with, and it usually takes time to become good at them. It will be a cumulative process over your undergraduate career. This is because different markers put emphases on different aspects of your report, although you can expect all markers to be alert to the basics, such as what goes in what sections. It is important, therefore, that you keep all your marked reports and refer to them on the next attempt.

Students frequently complain that the comments and feedback they get are inconsistent across different tutors or lecturers. Different staff members may have their pet peeves about specific aspects of conventions (I fuss about misplaced apostrophes, while some colleagues ignore them), so what is commented on in detail may vary from one marker to another. However, my experience has been that staff members go to extraordinary lengths to ensure that marking is consistent overall when several staff members are marking the same lab reports.

4.10 Summary

In conclusion, the following eight general points summarise the important steps you should follow when writing a psychology lab report:

1. Plan ahead to make best use of the time available.
2. Search for relevant references other than those given.
3. Be crystal clear about your hypotheses. Did the study test them? Did the results support them?
4. Write an outline of your study.

5 Get something comprehensive down on paper as soon as possible. This will usually be the Methods section.
6 Have someone critically read your first draft, and be prepared for a fair amount of rewriting. Also have someone critically read the revised draft before you type it up. Stick to the word limit.
7 Get your typed final presentation proofread for typos.
8 Get it in on time. If there is a genuine trauma, ask for an extension *before* the due date.

4.11 Checklist

For the first two or three reports that you write, you may find it helpful to check off these steps as you do them (although you may choose to do them in a different sequence to the one that follows):

Preparation

☐ Do you have all the handouts from your department (word limit, due date etc)?

☐ Do you have the details of the experimental design (i.e. what was done, how many subjects, groups, a copy of the questionnaire etc)?

☐ Have you read (obtained copies of) the references given?

☐ Have you decided on your hypothesis or hypotheses? This requires some critical evaluation of the references, unless you've been told what hypotheses are being tested. Are they specific and testable, written in terms of the variables as measured in your study? Did the study actually test them?

☐ Have you obtained more references with results relevant to your hypotheses? Again, some critical thinking needed, directed at these references.

☐ Have you calculated the appropriate statistics? Do they really test your hypotheses? Were the hypotheses supported?

Method (see p. 51)

☐ Do you have material covering the following subsections:
(a) Participants?
(b) Design?
(c) Materials (and/or Apparatus)?
(d) Procedure?

Results (see p. 58)

☐ Have you included a statement of how the data were processed?

☐ Does your report include descriptive statistics? Do you really need a table?

- ☐ Have you included a description of results of statistical tests?
- ☐ If you've used a table or figure, does it meet APA conventions?

Introduction (see p. 46)

- ☐ Have you included an opening statement of the area under consideration (but not a cliché)?
- ☐ Have you introduced the theoretical framework for the study, including relevant parts only of previous research, and defined terms where needed?
- ☐ Have you provided evidence that your reading of previous research has been critical, rather than just taking it at face value?
- ☐ Have you introduced the present study, stating the aims of it, and how it differs from previous research?
- ☐ Have you concluded with your operationalised hypotheses?

Discussion (see p. 69)

- ☐ Have you begun by stating whether the hypotheses were supported?
- ☐ How do the results relate to the previous research mentioned in the Introduction?
- ☐ What do the results *mean*? What are the implications for everyday life?
- ☐ Are there any methodological issues? Are problems systematic and observable in the results? If not, do you have a statement saying that there were no obvious methodological problems?
- ☐ Have you concluded with a brief summary of what you found, or a suggestion for correcting any problems you encountered?

Title page, Abstract, References (see pp. 42, 73)

- ☐ Have you produced a title page, and written an Abstract?
- ☐ Have you ensured that your Reference list includes all references cited, and meets APA conventions?

Presentation

- ☐ Rearrange the sections into the proper order.
- ☐ Did you have your first draft read by someone else? Was there anything that was unclear? What do you need to do to make it clear?
- ☐ Have you written a complete second draft? Is it clearer to someone else than the first one?
- ☐ Does the overall draft exceed the word limit? If so, cut it back.
- ☐ Have you typed it up? Have the entire report proofread. Correct any mistakes (white-out is acceptable!).
- ☐ If you are really keen, or really anxious, do as many more drafts as you can cope with!
- ☐ Keep a copy of the final, proofread version, either on disk or as a photocopy.

- ☐ Put the original into a manila folder, if expected to do so by your institution, with your details on the outside. Hand it in on time (or even early!).
- ☐ Celebrate a good job well done. You deserve it! (It's important to celebrate achievements.)

CHAPTER 5

essays in psychology

KEYWORDS
analytical categories, argument, evidence

IN THIS CHAPTER

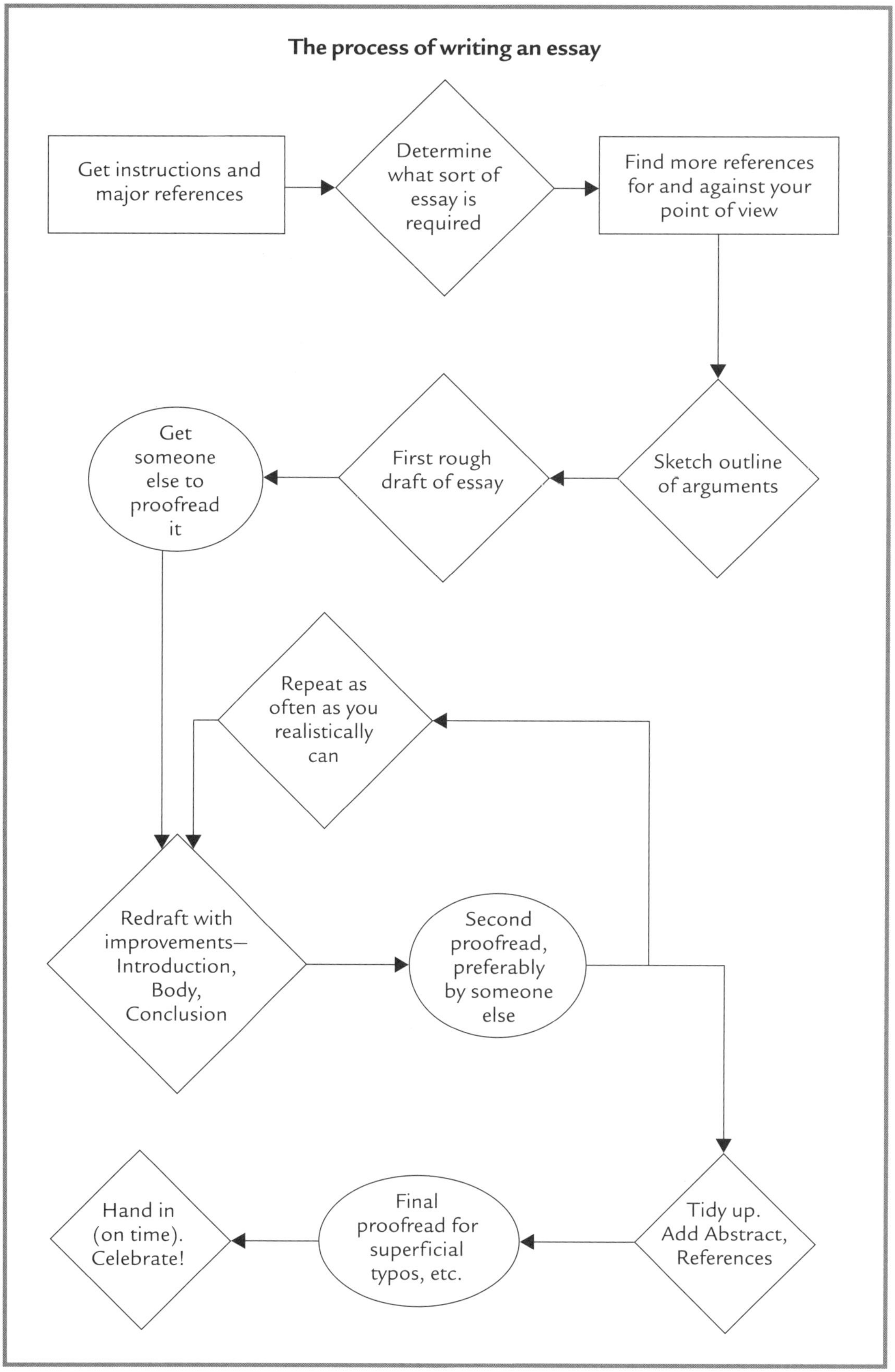
The process of writing an essay
Get instructions and major references
Determine what sort of essay is required
Find more references for and against your point of view
Sketch outline of arguments
First rough draft of essay
Get someone else to proofread it
Repeat as often as you realistically can
Redraft with improvements—Introduction, Body, Conclusion
Second proofread, preferably by someone else
Tidy up. Add Abstract, References
Final proofread for superficial typos, etc.
Hand in (on time). Celebrate!

5.1 How are essays different from lab reports?

ALTHOUGH CHAPTER 2 DEALT with the features that lab reports and essays have in common, the differences are considerable. For one thing, the conventions about format are not as strict, which allows you much more opportunity to be creative and to demonstrate your literary skill. Essays are not usually divided into sections the way lab reports are. Psychology essays shorter than about 2500 words do not usually include subheadings. That doesn't mean that there is no structure, but the structure is simpler and more flexible. Other than the Title page, Abstract, and Reference list, as long as there is an introduction, a body (or discussion, or argument) and a conclusion, you have met the requirements of format.

It is not really quite as simple as that. There is a clear sequence to writing the Introduction to a lab report because you are making a particular sort of argument – to justify the study you have supposedly run and the predictions you were testing. Although an essay is also an argument of a sort, usually to convince the reader that the weight of evidence points to a particular point of view, such an argument can be made in many different ways. As a student faced with an essay topic, one of the problems you must solve is to decide how to structure your argument. Since an essay doesn't report results which focus your attention on what has to be described and interpreted, you need to find a focus for yourself. To do this you need carefully to examine the question asked.

5.2 Choosing an essay topic

If you are fortunate, you will be given a choice of essay topic. How should you choose which one to do? When asked this, some students say they choose the one that looks easiest. This is a mistake. Markers adjust the severity of their marking according to the perceived difficulty of the topic. A question which is quite difficult to answer will be marked more leniently than one that is easier, so there is no advantage to choosing a topic just because it seems easy. To judge the difficulty of a topic, students often use as a criterion the directive words used in the question. There is a perception that essays that ask you to 'discuss' something are easier than those that ask you to 'critically evaluate'. This is not necessarily true. For any essay you are expected to critically evaluate what you read. Even a 'discuss' essay expects you to give arguments for and against a point of view. Finally, since you will be expected to do a fair bit of reading and thinking for any essay topic, you might as well choose an area that you are interested in or would like to learn more about.

While it is good to tackle a topic that interests you, be very careful of choosing an area in which you think you already have expert knowledge. If your brother suffers from dyslexia and you are therefore attracted to the essay question on this topic, be wary of making general statements on the basis of your single example. Your brother may not be typical. Many students, particularly mature age students, sometimes fall into the trap of writing about areas in which they have personal experience, and not always sticking to what the question asks of them. Be particularly careful of ideological hobby-horses. Although I'm happy to encourage passionate belief in a good cause, it is usually very difficult to write objectively about such a topic, or to stick to what the question requires.

I suggest that if you are given a list of choices, you reduce the possibilities to two or three topics which look interesting, then have a look at the references given for each and see how readable they are. Don't be too easily discouraged. Look at the reference lists of the articles you've been given and see if the journals cited are fairly easily accessible in your library, or those of nearby institutions. Having to chase after difficult-to-obtain references is a hassle that you should avoid unless you have a good study group which can apportion such hack work between its members.

5.3 Deciding what the essay topic asks

There are relatively few ways that essay topics are commonly worded in psychology. Table 21 gives examples of some of the sorts of essays that you might encounter in your first year or two of psychology. Look at the directive words in these topics, which are the words telling you to do something: discuss, evaluate, critically evaluate, critically review, compare and contrast, define, describe. It is important that your essay does what is asked of it, that is, that you answer what is asked, not what you might like to write about the topic in an ideal world. If it is not clear to you exactly what the question requires, talk to the lecturer who set the topic.

Table 21

Examples of Psychology Essay Titles

Discuss research into sibling relationships in children with a focus on the development of pro-social behaviour, jealousy and trust.

Discuss the role of deception in social psychological research. To what extent is deception a necessary methodological component of social psychological experiments?

What is the impact of genetic factors on the development of self-esteem or self-worth in adolescents? Discuss the evidence.

It is widely believed that ageing causes a decline in cognitive skills. Evaluate the assertion in relation to the experimental evidence on memory and skilled performance.

'Being an only child is a disease in itself.' Using current research, evaluate the accuracy of this statement made by the eminent American psychologist G. Stanley Hall.

Critically evaluate some of the evidence which suggests that under some conditions, rewarding people can actually cause them to become less motivated.

Developmental dyslexia is not a uniform disorder. Critically review the literature so as to illustrate the major sub-types of developmental dyslexia and the underlying cognitive and phonological deficits that have been identified with various types of dyslexia.

Compare and contrast the following theories of love: 'Love as attachment' and Sternberg's triangular theory of love.

Define, compare and contrast the concepts of 'conformity', 'compliance' and 'obedience'. Under what circumstances is conformity desirable and when is it undesirable social behaviour?

Describe the processes involved in solving the problem of the Hobbits and the Orcs in terms of the three-store memory model and IDEAL problem solving.

Anorexia nervosa is an eating disorder that affects an individual's physical as well as psychological health. What are the major theories of the etiology of *anorexia nervosa*?

The modern conception of companionate marriage puts heavy expectations on couples. What factors improve the odds of maintaining a satisfactory marital relationship? Support your assertions with research evidence.

Why do out-group members seem to 'all look alike'? Examine the reasons behind the perception of out-group homogeneity.

Critically examine research based on attribution theory into attributions of victim responsibility for rape. To what extent does such research support attribution theories and which attribution theories are most useful in this context?

Are males better equipped to be leaders than females? Critically assess whether it is just childhood interactions that influence leadership or whether other influences are involved.

'*Discuss*' means to describe evidence for and against the question under consideration. Typically you would find journal articles related to the topic, some in favour of, and some critical of that topic. For instance, the second example in Table 21 is about the role of deception in research. Some writers argue that deception is necessary, others that it should not be necessary; these writers suggest some alternatives to deception. Your essay should describe what these opposing viewpoints are, but, in view of the second sentence in the question, would then go on to look at why the proponents of deception say that deception is necessary.

'*Evaluate*' or '*critically evaluate*' is similar, but there is an expectation that you would end up with a judgment in favour of one side of the argument. You are being asked for an appraisal of the relative worth or weight of the opposing arguments. Here is a chance for you to express your personal opinion. However, don't get carried away. Markers are usually not impressed by dogmatic personal assertions. It is wiser to be tentative, and say, for example, 'It seems to me that . . .' or 'The weight of evidence seems to favour . . .'.

'*Review*' or '*critically review*' means to make a survey of the topic. Such an instruction usually expects a wide reading in the area. For many other instructions you might only need a fairly small number of references, but if you are asked to review an area, you must make an effort to get as wide a coverage of that area as possible in the time and with the resources available to you. You are expected briefly to summarise what various researchers have said, while being critical of poor arguments or methodological problems like small sample sizes or unrepresentative samples, or any other systematic biases that appear.

'*Compare*' or '*compare and contrast*' means that you are expected to look for similarities and differences between the theories or approaches described. Again, you are expected to be critical of what you read, but here you are not being asked to make a personal judgment between the two. You are really reporting what other authors have to say about the relative merits or disadvantages of the different approaches. You must come to some conclusion, at least about the importance or implications of major areas of similarity and difference.

'*Define*', '*describe*' and '*examine*' are instructions expecting you to present the information in some depth. '*Define*' means to say exactly what the term or phrase means. For example, if asked to define 'conformity' you would be expected to say that it is the tendency to change one's behaviour, attitudes, opinions, or even perceptions to match those of the bulk of others around you. You would also need to distinguish this tendency in particular situations from the more general personality trait of conformity. The further instruction to '*describe*' or '*examine*' means that you would go on to present a detailed account of the theory or term, and also present the implications they have for real life situations.

Note that all these directives expect you to be critical of what you read. This does not necessarily mean that you should be negative, but that, as I said in Chapter 2, you should apply critical thinking principles to what you read. Are the conclusions drawn by the authors reasonable on the basis of the evidence they report? It is perfectly acceptable to compliment authors on the representativeness of their sample or the imagination employed in operationalising some concept, just as it is to be critical of a small or unrepresentative sample, or an interpretation that ignores likely alternatives.

5.4 Preparation – reading, note-taking and planning

Having decided what the topic expects of you, you need to spend quite a lot of time in preparation. As you will find, if you ever come to construct a paved courtyard or renovate a house, the better the preparation the better the finished product, in this case your essay, will stand up to examination. For the typical psychology essay you will have been given only one or two references to start you off. You will already have skimmed through these in order to decide which topic to choose. Now read what your textbook has to say about the area in question. This will give you a general overview of what conventional thinking is on the subject, and will point you in the direction of further references. So will the reference lists of the articles you've been given.

With the question in mind, skim through those references that look as if they might be relevant. Take notes. Many students find it helpful to use a separate sheet of paper, or an index card for each article, and write the author(s), date, title, and journal details at the top of each sheet. This makes life easier when you come to acknowledgments in your essay and in writing your reference list. The notes you should take are the major points that the author(s) makes. This is often obvious from their Abstract, or from their subheadings. Many students photocopy anything that might appear even remotely useful. The danger here is that you end up with an indigestible mass of paper. Attaching summary notes to each article will help. Later, you can read the most relevant ones more thoroughly, highlighting important aspects of each.

Using these notes, you should then build an essay plan. If the directive is to 'compare and contrast' or 'evaluate' you might separate the references into heaps of 'for' and 'against'. If it is 'discuss' you might do the same, or you might organise them chronologically to show the evolution of thinking about the topic. You should then jot down the broad outline of what you intend your argument to be. You will eventually need an introduction and a conclusion, but the planning is primarily for the main body of the essay.

Now go back and read your references more thoroughly to flesh out the specific arguments you are going to make, or pieces of research you are going to describe. Here is where you should highlight parts of your photocopies. *Never* write on or highlight books that aren't your own. Make a copy of the relevant bits and write on or highlight that. Make a note of good page numbers on the summary sheet that you attached to the front of the article, or on stick-on 'Post-it' notes on the front page, or wherever relevant. As with lab reports, keep direct quotes to a minimum. It is always better to put the expression into your own words to indicate that you understand what is meant (acknowledging its source, of course!).

Now that you have a plan, start writing. You will probably find at first that it is pretty sketchy. That means that you will have to go back to your references again and again to find evidence to back up assertions that you are making, or to check the accuracy of your summaries of research. You may find that you need another look through *PsychInfo* or other sources to find more evidence to support some of your claims.

5.5 Structure of an essay

As mentioned above, the essay structure is to have a Title page, an Abstract, an Introduction, a body (or discussion), a conclusion and a Reference list. As I said about writing a lab report, it may be easier to write your first draft in a different order, in this case, drafting the body first, then the conclusion, then the introduction, and last of all the Abstract. However, I'll describe them in the order in which they will eventually be presented.

5.5.1 Title page and Abstract

The format of the Title page and Abstract is the same as for a lab report. Look back at section 4.1 for the details. Since the essay is not describing a study, you won't have information about participants and hypotheses in your Abstract. What you will summarise, in a maximum of 120 words, are the major arguments that led you to your conclusion. The conclusion itself should also be succinctly stated.

5.5.2 The Introduction

Although it comes first when you submit the final version, it is advisable to leave the writing of the Introduction until you have a reasonable draft of the essay body and conclusion. By then you know what you have argued and concluded, and can write an appropriate Introduction.

Opinions vary a bit on the format of Introductions, but one thing is clear: avoid wasting words with too general a statement. Similarly, although some map of the territory ahead is advisable, avoid too much detail too soon. Introductions to essays should not be longer than one long paragraph, perhaps 150 words or 10% of the word limit, whichever is less. The Introduction should not restate the title, but should say why the area being examined or evaluated is important or interesting. It should then go on to give the reader an idea of what you are going to argue. There are some examples of introductory paragraphs in Table 22, but be aware that they are not the only ways to introduce an essay.

Table 22

Examples of Introductory Paragraphs from Undergraduate Essays

Title: Critically examine some of the evidence which suggests that under some conditions, rewarding people can actually cause them to become less motivated.

While many people might consider that rewarding an individual for a particular activity would serve to enhance motivation, a number of studies have shown that under some conditions, rewarding people can actually cause them to become less motivated (Deci, 1971, 1972; Harackiewicz, Manderlink & Sansone, 1984; Lepper, Greene & Nisbett, 1973). This essay will describe the early studies of Deci, the criticisms of those studies by Lepper and colleagues, and the recent work by Harackiewicz and colleagues which attempted to address the earlier concerns, especially the variable of perceived control by the participant over the activity in question.

Title: Are males better equipped to be leaders than females? Critically assess whether it is just childhood interactions that influence the leadership potential of both sexes or whether there are any other influences involved.

Leadership has been traditionally regarded as a male domain (Dunlevy, 1991). Many theorists have attempted to explain the gender differences pertaining to leadership success (Singer, 1991). One such explanation has been offered by Maccoby (1990), a developmental theorist, who suggests that sex role differences occur primarily through childhood interactions. That is, during the childhood years, patterns of behaviour emerge that may be seen to better equip males than females to be leaders. Although childhood interactions seem to affect leadership potential, they are not the only influences involved in determining leadership success. Parental, teacher and media influences, workplace practices and expectations, and biological factors are also important considerations in any comprehensive attempt to explain gender differences in leadership.

Title: Discuss research evidence regarding the development of complex emotions in children.

A large proportion of the research on the emergence of emotions has focused on the development of the basic emotions in early infancy, which has resulted in the temporal development of the complex emotions being a comparatively uncharted area of study (Lewis, Sullivan, Stranger & Weiss, 1989). The general consensus seems to consider that happiness, interest, surprise, fear, anger, sadness, and disgust are the basic emotions, although there is still some debate as to whether disgust is an emotion or a reflex (Bootzin, Bower, Crocker & Hall, 1991). Complex emotions may be defined as those emotions that rely on an awareness of self, examples being

> jealousy, shame, embarrassment, envy, and pride (Lewis et al., 1989). In an attempt to trace the sequence of development of complex emotions, this essay will briefly examine the three alternative views of emotional development set out by Lewis et al. in their study of self-development and self-conscious emotions.

Title: Religion: Is it a source of increased acceptance of others, or a source of increased prejudice and intolerance?

> The popular maxim 'never discuss politics or religion' suggests that both topics, far from generating a lack of interest, generate much interest but much difference of opinion amongst people (Batson & Ventis, 1982). Because most religions preach unconditional love and acceptance of others, it has been presumed that religious people are generally less prejudiced than non-religious people (Herek, 1987). However, according to Batson (1976), major religions have often fostered doctrines leading to violent, inhumane and antisocial acts. Results of even the earliest studies (Allport & Kramer, 1946; Rosenblith, 1949) have revealed that religious involvement correlates positively with prejudice. This essay will critically evaluate the above claims in the light of subsequent research evidence.

Too much academic writing has a sort of detective novel structure – starting with the description of a problem, followed by a sort of gradual unfolding of information and evidence, leading up to a final burst of explanation at the end. In contrast, more journalistic styles tell the reader the important information at the very start, and gradually increase the level of detail, so that if some parsimonious sub-editor cuts the end off it to fit another advertisement in, the important information is still always there. While I don't wish to encourage you to be too journalistic in expression or use of evidence, the overall style is a good one. There is a lot to be said for making a statement of opinion in your Introduction, then using the body of the essay to justify that opinion. You may find that your lecturer or tutor is not all that happy with personal opinions. You can make it a little subtler by saying something like 'Evidence from Bloggs (1993) and Smith (1987) suggest that . . . is the case, in spite of some contrary evidence from Jones (1991).'

5.5.3 The body (discussion)

This is the largest section. Your essay plan is largely a plan for this section. Depending on the directive you've been given in the question, you will have a selection of previous research or theory to summarise, criticise, compare, or all three. The tricky part is deciding on the order in which this is to happen. Burdess (1991) talks about finding appropriate analytical categories, then dealing with each in turn. If you are comparing and contrasting approaches or theories, it is a good idea to deal with them one at a time, elaborating on their strengths, weaknesses, and areas of applicability.

If asked to critically evaluate a body of literature, the analytical categories might be particular pieces of research. In this case, the sequence could be chronological, since much research is cumulative and builds on previous work, and should improve with time. You can either point this out, or show how it isn't true. Alternatively you could write first about several pieces of research that support a point of view, then write about other research that doesn't support that viewpoint, or at least not so well, then come to some decision about what you believe on the basis of this evidence.

How much to include? One difficulty is deciding what material to include and what to omit. It is not unusual to feel that, since you have read an enormous amount of research, you must say something about everything you've read. Resist this temptation. It results in superficiality, since you will be aware that word limits are strictly enforced, and if you have a lot of things to talk about and limited space, you can only say a little about each. Your marker will be much more impressed with in-depth description and critical appraisal of a few references than a superficial treatment of many.

If you are having trouble reducing the amount of material you feel you need to talk about, you may be interpreting the question too broadly. It is usually acceptable in your introduction to say that an area is very broad and that the essay will deal with the concern in a particular context only. If you are in doubt about the wisdom of this approach for a particular essay, talk to the lecturer who set it.

Occasionally you may have the opposite problem. If you make an essay plan, write a first draft, correct and tidy it up, and are still far short of the word limit, then it is a signal that you need to do more reading. Have you described research in sufficient detail that the reader can see the logic of the conclusions reached or the criticisms made? Have you been fair in arguments for and against, or are your own prejudices showing? While it is acceptable, in fact expected, that you have an opinion, it is not acceptable to ignore evidence that you don't like! Even when you've written a proper length essay, these are shortcomings that should not be there!

Another problem in many student essays is the lack of linking sentences so that paragraphs flow logically. Such essays are a collection of largely unrelated paragraphs. You need to have a sentence at the end of one paragraph that leads the reader to anticipate what the next paragraph may be about. Alternatively, your first sentence in a new paragraph should suggest why that particular new paragraph is placed after the previous one. This can be done as simply as starting a new paragraph with 'In contrast, Jones (1992) found that . . .' and using that paragraph to deal with a different idea from that in the previous paragraph. Alternatively, if you wish to enlarge on one study in one paragraph, and someone else's work in the next paragraph, you might say 'Additional support for this idea comes from Bloggs's (1993) study, where . . .'. This is what I have done with this paragraph and the preceding one.

The body of the essay will be the major part. As I mentioned before, the Introduction should not be more than about 150 words. The conclusion should be similar in length, about 150 words, and certainly not more than about 10% of the word limit. So if your word limit is 1500 words, the body of the essay should be about 1200 of them. Don't be paranoid about counting them, but use these ideas as a guide.

5.5.4 The conclusion

The conclusion is a summary of the major points of your argument, or a final statement of your opinion, having evaluated conflicting, or at least comprehensive evidence. What you have to do is find a balance between an abrupt ending which looks like you just ran out of ideas, and a repetition of points that you seem to have just made, particularly in a fairly short essay. It is usually only a paragraph long, and it should not introduce any new material or ideas.

The main reason that students have difficulty with conclusions is that they seem not to have opinions about the material. Once you have seriously addressed the critical reading of other work, you should find that you do have an opinion on the area under question. The conclusion is the place to state it, remembering that even here you need to back up your opinion with evidence. Since I've just said not to introduce new material, you need to refer back to work in the body of the essay, even if only by name and date. Table 23 has several examples of concluding paragraphs.

Table 23

Examples of Concluding Paragraphs from Undergraduate Essays ✓

Title: The facial feedback hypothesis suggests that the experience of a particular emotion can follow from a particular facial expression. Laird has used the manipulation of facial muscles to induce specific emotions as an independent variable in experiments. Critically evaluate some of this literature, and evaluate how effective you think the method has been.

> In summary, existing research on the muscle by muscle technique of testing the facial feedback hypothesis is contradictory. However, so many faults have been pointed out by researchers such as Buck (1980) and Tourangeau and Ellsworth (1979), and many of the arguments for the hypothesis are so weak that those studies which showed positive results are unconvincing. Obviously more research needs to be done, particularly using between-subjects designs, but the muscle by muscle technique studies that have been carried out so far simply appear to contain too many methodological flaws to be considered effective.

Title: How do the gender stereotypes we hold affect our interaction with a member of the opposite sex? Critically evaluate some of the recent research in this area.

In conclusion, recent research has indicated that differences in behavioural style do exist between men and women when interacting with each other. These behavioural differences are parallel to and influenced by gender stereotypes. Whether the stereotypes are accurate or not, they function as part of sex role expectations, and so influence the behaviour of men and women. An understanding of the differences in interaction styles, and the stereotypes that pervade and direct them can be helpful in overcoming misunderstandings between the sexes and so narrow the communication gap of the gender divide.

Title: Are there gender-specific differences in the ways in which parental socialisation influences the development of empathy in children?

Overall, the proposition that there are gender-specific differences in the influence of parental socialisation on the development of empathy in children could be considered highly controversial. In previous research there is both a lack of consistency in findings, and a lack of control for, and consideration of, numerous possible confounding influences. Although the existing literature tends to favour the notion that mothers are particularly influential in developing greater empathic understanding and responsiveness in their daughters, the validity of this finding is questionable on the basis of the limitations and problems discussed above.

Title: Discuss findings from psychological research into attention-deficit hyperactivity disorder in the context of information-processing approaches to cognitive development.

In summary, information processing approaches to cognitive development provide a clear framework which enables psychological researchers to direct research and systematically explore the inattentive behaviour demonstrated by ADHD children, since further investigation is required into the competencies and deficits displayed by such children. Exploration into the relationships between cognitive processes and the academic and social difficulties that ADHD children experience may ultimately suggest specific intervention techniques to assist these children.

5.5.5 References

The Reference list at the end of an essay is formatted in exactly the same way as for a lab report, so look back at section 4.6. In-text referencing is also the same as for a lab report, and this was dealt with in section 2.6. You may find markers slightly more lenient as to what counts as evidence for an essay compared with a lab report. For instance, a newspaper article would certainly indicate current interest in a particular topic and that may be a valid point in an essay, whereas you would never reference a newspaper article in a lab report. Don't get carried away, though. Avoid references to radio or television programs in essays, however interesting or topical they may be. A newspaper is acceptable, because it is a reference that can be checked upon. Usually it is not practical for an interested reader to check on what a radio or television program said, so as a standard of evidence it is not very good.

Students sometimes complain that although they've referred to many references they haven't received as good a grade as a friend who used fewer. As with lab reports, there are no firm rules about the number of references to use, but generally speaking it is better to write sensibly about a few references than to be promiscuous with many. When reading the references you've found, you will often find that many of them say the same things. It is not necessary to make a general statement then put six references in brackets, unless you are specifically making the point that the statement is a well-supported one. Your marker is more interested in your critical evaluation of any particular reference than in the fact that you've read six of them. Check with the lecturer or tutor who set the question, but as a rule of thumb, a first-year essay should not require more than about six or eight references, and a second-year essay should not require more than about 12 references. Some lecturers are happy with fewer, especially if they are asking you to criticise a particular author's thoughts on a topic.

5.6 Redrafting and presentation

As with a lab report, redrafting is crucial. When you have a first draft written, however brief, congratulate yourself. Then get someone else to cast an eye over it for you, with a view to pointing out areas which lack clarity or contain poor argument, or insufficient evidence to back up assertions. Look back at section 2.7 for more information about redrafting.

Presentation is the same as for a lab report. As I said in section 2.9, most institutions these days expect your assignments to be typed, double spaced, with wide margins, and submitted in a folder with your name, your tutor's name (please spell it correctly!) and the day and time of your lab class.

Finally, get it in on time. Try to get it completed 48 hours early, so that last minute hassles with computers can be overcome, or at least addressed. Back up each draft on a separate floppy, so you always have the previous draft you wrote available if something terrible happens to your final draft. Reward yourself for keeping to your schedule. It *is* hard, so when successful in sticking to your timing, you've earned a special treat. Psychology staff often put more emphasis on due dates than staff in other subjects, and that is because psychology is an accredited course leading (eventually) to a professional vocation where time is important. However, if you have a genuine, documentable reason for an extension, don't be afraid to ask *before* the due date.

5.7 Further reading

There are several books available that address essay writing in the social sciences, and your library will probably have copies of them. Although none of these were specifically written for psychology students, they contain much good advice. Ones that I have found to be especially useful are:

Betts, K., & Seitz, A. (1994). *Writing essays and research reports in the social sciences.* (2nd ed.). Melbourne: Thomas Nelson.

Burdess, N. (1991). *The handbook of student skills for the social sciences and humanities.* Sydney: Prentice Hall.

Marshall, L.A., & Rowland, F. (1998). *A guide to learning independently.* (3rd ed.). Melbourne: Longman Cheshire.

All these books are by Australian academics for Australian students. Burdess's book is particularly good on general study skills such as preparing for lectures and tutorials, taking notes, examination techniques and general writing skills. Marshall and Rowland's book is very good for making it clear that studying at university is different from studying at school. I found it valuable as a mature age student coming back to study after many years away from it. Betts and Seitz's book is especially good on essays.

5.8 Checklist

For the first two or three essays that you write, you may find it helpful to plan your time, then to check off these steps as you do them (although you may choose to do them in a different sequence to the one that follows):

Preparation

- ☐ Do you have all the handouts from your department (word limit, due date, etc)?
- ☐ Have you chosen an essay topic?
- ☐ Have you read (obtained copies of) the references given?
- ☐ Are you clear on what the topic is asking you to do (Evaluate? Discuss?)?
- ☐ Have you obtained enough references to allow you to have a reasonable opinion on the area in question?
- ☐ Have you read them critically, taking appropriate notes?
- ☐ Have you jotted down an essay plan – at least the rough sequence in which you are going to argue your case?

Body of the essay (see p. 94)

- ☐ Have you listed the arguments *for* your case?
- ☐ What about the arguments *against*?
- ☐ Are you confident of backing up your opinion with evidence?

Conclusion (see p. 96)

- ☐ Can you fairly state the reaasons for your decisions?
- ☐ Is it a single brief paragraph?

Introduction (see p. 92)

- ☐ Have you begun by stating the area under question and your opinion?
- ☐ Have you given the reader/marker a verbal map of what to expect in the way of your argument?
- ☐ Is it brief (not more than about 150 words)?

Title page, Abstract, References (see pp. 42, 73, 97)

- ☐ Have you produced a title page, and written an Abstract?
- ☐ Have you ensured that your Reference list includes all references cited, and meets APA conventions?

Presentation

- ☐ Rearrange the sections into the proper order.
- ☐ Did you have your first draft read by someone else? Was there anything that was unclear? What do you need to do to make it clear?
- ☐ Have you written a complete second draft? Is it clearer to someone else than the first one?
- ☐ Does the overall draft exceed the word limit? If so, cut it back.
- ☐ Have you typed it up? Have the entire report proofread. Correct any mistakes (white-out is acceptable!).
- ☐ If you are really keen, or really anxious, do as many more drafts as you can cope with!
- ☐ Keep a copy of the final, proofread version, either on disk or as a photocopy.
- ☐ Put the original into a manila folder, with your details on the outside. Hand it in on time (or even early!).
- ☐ Celebrate a good job well done. You deserve it!

CHAPTER 6

USING THE INTERNET AS A RESOURCE

KEYWORDS
empirical, evidence

IN THIS CHAPTER

THE INTERNET CAN BE a valuable resource when preparing for a lab report or essay in psychology, but it can be very frustrating to use. It is valuable because there is an enormous amount of information, from basic textbook content and related materials, to electronic journal articles on a multitude of subject areas. It can be frustrating because there is an awful lot of rubbish there too, and it can take up a lot of your time sorting through the chaff to get a few grains of wheat that are useful for your assignment.

6.1 Lab reports

For lab reports, my advice is to stick to your textbook and a dictionary of psychology to define the major areas addressed by your study, and to use the journal articles which are easily available in your own library for evidence of previous studies in those areas. *Only use the Internet to access electronic copies of journals* not otherwise available in your library. I say this because psychological reports are concerned with deciding whether there is sufficient evidence for making the claims (hypotheses) that researchers put forward about human thought and behaviour. The quality of that evidence is important. The scientific method accepts only some sorts of evidence, primarily objective, observable, repeatable data. This type of data has usually been reported in reputable journals, and it has been accepted into those journals through a process of peer review. Other sorts of information, such as the opinions of philosophers, novelists, journalists and anyone else who can put information onto the web, can certainly be valuable in deciding what to study, what sort of problems should be addressed and what kind of questions might be asked. Such questions, however, are *not* usually considered to be evidence, and so do not normally have a place in an undergraduate lab report.

In summary, I suggest that for lab reports you simply use the Internet as another way to access psychological journals, and in the body of your report, you reference what you cite in the same way as any other journal article. In the Reference list you use the format I described on page 77.

6.2 Essays

Psychological essays allow wider scope in the use of material available on the Internet. The Internet provides the means for expressing varying and interesting opinions which demonstrate the concerns currently occupying the minds of writers, researchers and others.

Again, however, it is important to be aware of the quality of evidence that is represented. It is crucial that you make clear whether you are reporting a matter of opinion, or the result of research. If it is research, has it been reviewed by the authors' peers in the discipline, or is it the academic equivalent of vanity publishing ('none of the journals would accept it, so I put it on the web myself')?

Referencing The importance of referencing what you cite in a lab report or essay is to enable your reader or marker to go to the reference and see whether you are accurately reporting what the original author said. The nature of the Internet sometimes makes that difficult, since the content of many web pages can, and is, often changed. For that reason, your Reference list should include not only the web address (URL), but also the date you accessed it. However, if the material is in a web page which is likely to change, I recommend that you don't use it. See section 4.6.3 for details of referencing an Internet site.

How do you use Internet material? In an essay, the way you might use Internet material is to report that a particular topic is popular, in the sense of having many entries. You might briefly describe some of them. You would need to be critical in the sense of recognising whether the material is a matter of opinion, or the result of empirical study. Depending on the way the essay question is framed, you may argue for or against the opinions expressed, using evidence from other reading or research. Alternatively, you might use the Internet to familiarise yourself with a topic, especially if your library has few resources in that area. It might allow you to narrow the scope of your enquiry, and possibly discover some of the names of researchers current in the field, whose formal publications you can then access. The possibilities are limited only by your imagination, as long as you remember to acknowledge the work of others by properly citing them in your report.

6.3 General resources

Having said all that, the web is great for generally exploring a topic, and frequently contains material that is more current than journals, and much more current than books. That is because almost all universities have web sites, and many academics maintain their own pages discussing their current research, often with links to related material. Here are some web addresses that you may like to explore. I've checked them all in July 2002, and all were active then. You may want to use a search engine to find a specific topic, and that is fine, but usually results in lots of extraneous material that is time consuming to wade through.

Your textbook publisher will also have a web site, usually with links to ancillary material relevant to that text, and probably including study guides and examples of test questions. Such sites are very well worth exploring. The companion website for this book, which contains interactive exercises to help you master the conventions we demand of you, is:

www.prenhall.com/findlay_au

Another address that supports selected introductory psychology texts is:

http://www.prenhall.com/livepsych/

Here are sites maintained by the peak bodies of psychology in Australia and America:

Australian Psychological Society: http://www.aps.psychsociety.com.au
American Psychological Association: http://www.apa.org

These sites have a lot of information relevant to professional psychologists, which won't be of immediate relevance to you, although they will give you a flavour of what is important to psychologists, but they do have links to student resources.

I'm a bit reluctant to give just a few sites, in case they are somehow thought to be special. They aren't. They are just ones I've found when I've been looking. There are plenty more out there to be found, and they may well be better than these. However, having said that, here is one site, which has copies of some of the most famous papers in the history of psychology, and which allows you to search them by author or topic:

http://psychclassics.yorku.ca/

A site for information within the general area of social psychology is:

http://www.socialpsychology.org/

A similar site devoted to aspects of the psychology of personality is:

http://pmc.psych.nwu.edu/personality.html

A site which leads to a lot of information about online journals in psychology is:

http://www.psych-central.com/online.htm

Happy searching (but don't get carried away!).

Appendix A
Sample of a good lab report

I have included two sample lab reports in this edition. I have always been hesitant to include these sample reports. In the case of the example of a good lab report I did not want students to think that there was only one way of writing a lab report, or of expressing particular aspects of one. However, I was persuaded as it seemed desirable to have a graphic index. If you are after a quick reference for something and know it belongs in, say, the Introduction, but can't think of a word to allow you to look up the real index, you can quickly and easily find what you want from the sample lab report. *The numbers referred to in the boxes are the chapter, section and subsection numbers in this book.* Please bear in mind that this sample report is a fairly simple one. By second-year your reports will be longer and more complex, so don't use it as a template, simply as a way to find what you want in the body of the book.

This is the first edition of this book to show an example of a badly written lab report. Again I have previously hesitated to include one for the same reason that students sometimes have trouble evaluating the goodness of their own writing—once in print, the neatness of presentation overwhelms the critical sense. However, I hope that the abundant sprinkling of numbers in superscript, indicating that something is wrong, will alert you to the shortcomings. The numbers refer to notes on pages 119–121 explaining just *what* is wrong. Please note that such a system of numbers indicating notes should *not* be used in your own lab reports, even though you will occasionally see them in published articles. The other important thing to note is that this poor example is unusually short, even for a first-year lab report. It is only there to give you an example of all the things you should not do, and since I found 83 of them, that should be enough of a dire warning!

The Effect of a Concurrent Verbal Task on a Unimanual Skill

Jenny Tan

Title 4.1

Submitted as a Psychology 101 Practical Report
Due Date: 18th September 2003
Tutor: Gordana Bruce
Class: Friday 1:30–3:30

Note no page number

Abstract 4.1

Abstract

This study examined the effect of a concurrent verbal task on a unimanual skill. Undergraduate psychology students (102 females and 82 males, mean age 24.2 years) each balanced a dowel rod on either their right or left index finger, with and without concurrently repeating a short phrase. The order of tasks was counterbalanced. The hypothesis that right-handed males would experience shorter right-handed, but not left-handed, balancing times while verbalising, was supported. The results also supported the prediction that right-handed females would experience little difference in balancing times for either hand, whether they balanced while verbalising or in silence. It was concluded that males, presumably more hemispherically specialised, experience interference effects which are not experienced by the less hemispherically lateralised females.

Numbers 4.4.3

Note: The APA *Manual* does not specify where on the page the Abstract should go. I think it looks better centred vertically, but some academics prefer to see it at the top of the page. Check with your tutor or lecturer to ascertain their preference.

Note no page number

Introduction 4.2

The effect of a concurrent verbal task on a unimanual skill

Title at top of page p. 42

Jenny Tan

General opening statement p. 45

The laterality of cerebral function and the duality of the brain have been issues of interest dating back to early Egyptian times, and to the writings of Hippocrates (Dimond & Beaumon, 1974), and are still of considerable interest to neuropsychologists (McCourt 2002). Dimond and Beaumon also cite the work of Sir Thomas Browne, who, in 1648 first discussed the possibility that different hemispheres of the brain controlled different sides of the body. Simon and Sussman (1987) suggested that there may well be interference with a task performed by a particular hand if language and motor functions were to be controlled by the same hemisphere of the brain. In most people, particularly right-handers, speech is controlled by the left hemisphere, which also controls the right hand (Sdorow, 1993).

'&' or 'and' p. 18

In-text referencing 2.6

Kinsbourne and Cook (1971) tested the possibility of such interference. They predicted that the activity of balancing a dowel on the right index finger would be intefered with by concurrent verbalisation. Using a sample only of right-handed subjects, Kinsbourne and Cook found that shorter right-hand balancing times were observed when the subjects verbalised than when they were silent. The researchers concluded that hemispheric sharing generated mutual interference between the activities of balancing and verbalising.

Referral to same authors within a paragraph p. 18

Overview of prior research p. 47

A study using female as well as male subjects, and balancing on both right and left index fingers was reported by Johnson and Kozma (1977). They found similar results for right-handed males, but found little difference for right-handed females between the verbal and non-verbal conditions. Johnson and Kozma suggested that this was because the language function was less clearly lateralised in females.

Introducing the present study p. 50

The present study was designed to replicate and extend the study of Kinbourne and Cook (1971), by including a measure of handedness, as well as using both male and female subjects. It was hypothesised that for right-handed males there would be a shorter mean right-hand balancing time with concurrent verbalising than without, but that mean left-hand balancing times would be unaffected. It was also predicted that for right-handed females, mean balancing times on both hands would be unaffected by verbalising when performing the same tasks.

Hypotheses p. 50, Tables 3, 9

Page numbering starts here with page 2

Method 4.3

2

Method

Method does not normally start on a new page

Participants 4.3.1, Table 10

Participants

Note italics, no period

The sample consisted of 184 undergraduate psychology students who completed the study as part of a course requirement. There were 103 females (M = 25.0 years, SD = 9.1 years) and 82 males (M = 24.2 years, SD = 8.8 years). One hundred and forty eight of the subjects were right handed, and it is only their results which will be reported in this study.

Italicise letters representing statistics p. 57

Materials 4.3.3

Materials

Handedness was determined using an adaptation of the Edinburgh Handedness Inventory (EHI) developed by Oldfield (1970). This inventory is a 10-item questionnaire asking which hand participants used for various common tasks, such as writing or opening a box lid. A laterality quotient was calculated for each participant, as suggested by Oldfield. A copy of the EHI is included as Appendix A.

Abbreviations p. 56, Table 12

Summary of scales p. 55, Table 11

Reference to Appendix p. 55

A wooden dowel rod (12 mm diameter × 45 cm long) was used as the object to be balanced. There were four versions of the instruction sheet (included as Appendix B). Each version indicated the sequence of four practice trials and 20 experimental trials. The 20 experimental trials consisted of various orders of the following four balancing tasks: right finger, silent (RS); right finger, verbal (RV); left finger, silent (LS); and left finger, verbal (LV). The verbal task consisted of subjects continually repeating a short phrase such as 'the child is running' whilst concurrently balancing the dowel rod on an index finger.

Procedure 4.3.4

Procedure

Class participants completed the EHI, and were than randomly allocated to pairs, with the exception that given the ratio of males to females, males in a male/female pair were required to be the subject rather than the experimenter. Four 1-minute, non-verbal practice trials were conducted. Subjects then performed the 20 experimental trials, the sequence of which was counterbalanced for order of hand used, and whether verbalisation was concurrent or not. For each trial, the time the subject was able to keep the dowel balanced on their index finger was measured in seconds, and recorded. Instructions were in writing and were presented verbally by the 'experimenter' to each subject individually.

Counter-balancing p. 58

Results 4.4

Note that Results does not *have* to start on a new page

3

Results

Report any effects of counter-balancing p. 58

There was very little mean difference in handedness quotient between males and females, and no differences in mean length of time balanced across various orders of trials. Mean laterality quotient from the EHI, the mean balancing times for the four conditions are summarised in Table 1. The results indicate that, as predicted, mean right-handed balancing times for right-handed males were noticeably shorter when verbalising than when silent, yet there was little difference in mean times between these conditions for left-hand balancing. For female subjects, verbalising appeared to have little effect on mean balancing times for either hand.

Introduction of Tables p. 62, Table 15

Tables 4.4.5

Leave reasonable space before a table

Table titles pp. 62–63 Table 16

Table 1

Means and Standard Deviations of Balancing Times and Handedness Quotient for Right-handed Participants

Sex	RS (secs)	RV (secs)	LS (secs)	LV (secs)	Handedness quotient	*n*
Females	8.7 (9.5)	7.9 (7.8)	5.2 (4.6)	5.2 (4.1)	73.1	77
Males	21.6 (17.4)	15.6 (11.2)	11.4 (11.3)	10.2 (6.4)	75.4	71

Notes: Figures in brackets are standard deviations
RS = right-hand, silent; RV = right-hand, verbal; LS = left-hand, silent; LV = left-hand, verbal.

Note there are no vertical lines

Notes to tables p. 63

Leave reasonable space after a table

Discussion 4.5

Note that Discussion does not start on a new page

Discussion

State whether hypotheses are supported p. 68

The results of the study supported the hypotheses for both right handed males and females. Right-handed males did experience shorter mean right-hand balancing times when concurrently verbalising than when silent. In contrast, right handed males experienced little impairment in mean balancing times for their left hand, whether verbalising or silent. There was little difference in mean balancing times for females between the verbal and silent conditions for either hand.

4

Support for prior research pp. 68–69

The findings for the males support the results of Kinsbourne and Cook (1971) and Johnson and Kozma (1977). Since the present study used a considerably larger sample than either of these studies, the results provide good evidence that interference with right-sided motor control by the left hemisphere of the brain due to the concurrent verbal activity did contribute to impaired performance for right-handed males. That right-handed females suffered no such comparable impairment is also consistent with the results of Johnson and Kozma (1977). These findings would seem to provide additional support for the suggestion that language function is more bilateral in females.

Possible methodological concerns pp. 70–71

One systematic bias observable in the results is that males in general achieved longer balancing times. This may well be due to the greater experience they have with similar physical activities. Another systematic bias, also to be expected, was that balancing times were consistently shorter for the non-preferred hand. However, this effect appeared not to influence the testing of the hypotheses.

Implications of results for everyday life p. 71

The results of the present study imply that right-handed males in particular will experience interference when attempting to concurrently verbalise and perform a unimanual skill with their right hand. It would appear that such interference is determined by factors such as gender and probably handedness. Such knowledge may assist people in choices and decisions regarding the allocation of tasks to males or females. Knowing about the probability of such interference might also influence the appropriate timing of discussions or conversations with manual workers, or the combining of skills that may be impaired by hemispheric interference.

Concluding paragraph p. 71

In conclusion, this study examined the effect of concurrent verbalisation on the motor function of balancing a dowel on an index finger. The results indicated that right-handed males, but not females, experienced shorter right hand balancing times when verbalising than when silent. For left hand balancing, neither sex experienced a difference in balancing times between the silent or verbalising conditions. Consequently, it appears that for people with strongly lateralised language function, an interference effect occurs when they verbalise at the same time as performing a right-handed task, such that the quality of the task performance is impaired.

References 4.6

5

References

Reference list *does* begin on a new page

Format of books 4.6.1

Format of journal articles 4.6.2

Later editions 4.6.1

Dimond, S.J., & Beaumon, J.G. (1974). *Hemisphere function in human brain.* London: Paul Elek (Scientific Books).

Johnson, O., & Kozma, A. (1977). Effects of concurrent verbal and musical tasks on a unimanual skill. *Cortex, 13*, 11–16.

Kinsbourne, M., & Cook, J. (1971). Generalised and lateralised effects of concurrent verbalisation on a unimanual skill. *Quarterly Journal of Experimental Psychology, 23*, 341–345.

McCourt, F. (2002). *Class notes for neuropsychology 486.* Retrieved September 1, 2002 from http://www.psychology.psych.ndsu.nodak.edu/mccourt/website/htdocs/HomePage/Psy486/Cerebral%20Asymmetry/Cerebral%20asymmetry.html.

Oldfield, R.C. (1971). The assessment and analysis of handedness: The Edinburgh inventory. *Neuropsychologia, 9*, 97–113.

Sdorow, L.M. (1993). *Psychology* (2nd ed.). Dubuque, Iowa: Brown & Benchmark. Chapter 3.

Simon, T.J., & Sussman, H.M. (1987). The dual task paradigm: Speech dominance or manual dominance? *Neuropsychologia, 25*, 559–569.

Note: You would not normally include a reference like the McCourt (2000) one, but I wanted to include a current Internet reference in order to show you how it is referenced.

Appendix B
Sample of a poor lab report

Hemispheric Lateralisation[1]

Jenny Tan

Psych 101

2

3

[4] This study looked at the effect of hemisheric lateralization[5] in psychology students[6] who balanced dowel rods on right or left index fingers.

[7]

This was a replication[8] of Kinsbourne and Cook's (1971) study, which found interference.[9] Subjects[10] balanced rods on right and left index fingers, while either talking or not talking. We[11] found interference effects[12] for males but not for females, as expected.[13]

1[14]

Introduction[15]

[16]Kinsbourne &[17] Cook (1971) found that balancing a dowel rod on the finger could be interfered with[18] if subjects[19] talked at the same time. This was because the left hemisphere controls the right side of the body, and also controls speech.[20]

Johnson[21] and Kozma (1977) also studied balancing with females as well as males.[22] they[23] found the same results as Cook and Kinsbourne[24] [25] for males, but found no difference for females.[26]

[27]

Our[28] study replicated Kinsbourne and Cook (1971)[29] but was extended because we made allowance for whether the subject was right-handed or left-handed. This was because of brain lateralization.[30] The hypothesis is that right-handed males will[31] have interference when talking and balancing on their right index finger[32], but not their left, but right-handed females will not have any interference for either hand.[33]

[34]

Method[35] [36]

Participants.[37]

Participants consisted of 103 females[38] (M = 25.0, SD = 9.1)[39] [40] and 82 males (M= 24.2, SD = 8.8).[41]

Materials

The EHI (Oldfield, 1970) was used to test handedness. It has 10 items asking what hand is used to do various tasks. [42, 43, 44]

Dowel rods were used for balancing.[45]

The tasks were: balance on right index finger, no talking; balance on right finger, talking; balance on left finger, no talking; balance on left finger, talking.[46, 47]

[48]

Participants filled in the EHI, and were put in pairs[49]. There were 4[50] practice trials without talking, then 20 experimental trials.[51] The time in seconds[52] was measured, and instructions were given by the person not doing the balancing.[53]

Results[54, 55]

Table 1
Means and standard deviations of balancing times and handedness quotient for right-handed participants.[56, 57]

Sex	RS	RV	LS	LV	Handedness	n
Females	8.7 (9.5)	7.9 (7.8)	5.2 (4.6)	5.2 (4.1)	73.1	77
Males	21.6 (17.4)	15.6 (11.2)	11.4 (11.3)	10.2 (6.4)	75.4	71

[58, 59, 60]

Table 1 shows the results are much shorter for males using right hand when talking, (15.6 vs 21.6)[61] but left hand times are not very different (11.4 vs 10.2).[62] For females the times are not very different for talking or not talking. However, times are shorter for left hand balancing than for right hand balancing (males 11.4, 10.2, vs 15.6 or 21.6) females, 5.2, vs 7.9, 8.7). This supports the hypothesis.[63]

Discussion

The hypothesis was supported.[64] Males[65] balanced the dowel for shorter times on their right hands (15.6)[66,67] than on their left (21.6) when talking, but females had almost the same time.[68]

Kinsbourne and Cook (1971) and Johnson and Kozma (1977) supported these findings[69], since they also found males balanced longer[70] when not talking, and Johnson and Kozma found females did not show a difference by hand.[71]

This is because[72] in males the language function is strongly located in the left hemisphere which also controls the right hand, and so if they are talking and balancing on the right hand, there is interference because the brain is trying to do too much, whereas women have language distributed across both hemispheres, so any interference is equal on both hands.[73]

Both males and females showed shorter times using their left hand[74]. This is because they are right handed. Men showed longer times because they are more used to physical things.[75]

The implications for the real world[76] are that males who are strongly right-handed will not be as good at manual tasks with their right hand if they are talking at the same time. This could apply to men in factories.[77]

Problems with this study are that it was just done on students, instead of a representative sample.[78]

In summary, strongly right-handed males showed an interference effect when balancing a dowel on their right index finger and talking at the same time.[79]

References[80]

Johnson, O., & Kozma, A. (1977). Effects of concurrent verbal and musical tasks on a unimanual skill. *Cortex,* 13, 11-16.[81, 82]

Kinsbourne, M., & Cook, J. (1971). Generalised and lateralised effects of concurrent verbalisation on a unimanual skill. *Quarterly Journal of Experimental Psychology,* 23, 341-345.

[83]

Problems:

1 Titles should be in normal, that is, 12-point font, and should not be underlined. Similarly, the title page should not have borders or decorations.
2 There should be sufficient information to allow your tutor to return the report to you, i.e., day and time of tutorial class. See the good example on p. 105
3 The Abstract should be labelled "Abstract". All sections of the laboratory report should be double-spaced.
4 The first line of Abstracts should *not* be indented.
5 "looked at hemispheric lateralization" is too vague. You need to say that it was the effect of hemispheric lateralization on interference with a balancing task while speaking. Also, be consistent in spelling. It doesn't matter which, but decide if you'll use the Australian "s" or the American "z" in words like utilise.
6 There should be adequate description of participants, i.e., at least how many, and possibly ages or other demographics.
7 The Abstract should be a single paragraph.
8 If you must have a reference, it should read "an extension of" since we also checked for handedness. Some academics don't like to see references in the Abstract. There is no APA rule, but you *should* be able to describe the study without them.
9 "found interference" is too vague. You need to be more explicit.
10 The preferred term is "participants". See section 4.3.1, p. 53
11 Avoid personal pronouns. It would be better to say "Results indicated…"
12 Again, too vague. Since you only have 120 words you cannot afford to be repetitive, but you must be explicit.
13 You need a concluding statement.

Overall, the Abstract needs to describe aims, method, hypotheses, results, and a conclusion.

14 Do *not* show a page number on the first page.
15 The Introduction does *not* have a title.
16 You should have an introductory statement describing why this area is interesting or important to report on. In fact, it would be better to have a whole introductory paragraph describing the idea of different parts of the brain controlling different functions.
17 You need to know when to use "and" (outside brackets) and when to use "&" (inside them). See section 2.6, p. 18.
18 Again, "interfered with" is too general. Say that length of time a dowel could be balanced was shorter when the participant talked concurrently.
19 Participants, not subjects.
20 Be careful with dogmatic statements. Better to say that Kinsbourne and Cook (1971) suggested that this was the reason.
21 You should indent the start of a new paragraph.
22 "balancing with females as well as males" is ambiguous. Who balanced what?
23 Remember to start new sentence with an uppercase letter.
24 Here the order of the authors is reversed. It is important that you get the order correct. See section 4.6, p. 73
25 Since this is the first time these authors are mentioned in this paragraph, you should also include the date of publication.
26 Again, be explicit. What difference was not found? If you have been careful in wording the earlier part of this sentence, this would be clear.
27 Even in a very first 1st year lab report, you need much more description of prior research to justify what you end up hypothesising. You should describe in some detail what Kinsbourne and Cook (1971) and Johnson and Kozma (1977) *did* in order to come up with their conclusions. See the good example!

28 Again, don't say "our study" say "the present study".

29 It wasn't Kinsbourne and Cook that you replicated (we're not into cloning!), but their study. Say so.

30 Too vague! You should have had a paragraph describing why handedness is relevant.

31 Hypotheses should be in the past tense - you are reporting what has already been done.

32 Ambiguous. It reads as if the participants are each balancing on their own index fingers. I'm not sure I'd get *that* past the ethics committee!

33 Again, be more specific. It would be more interpretable if your previous paragraph had described the importance of handedness. Also you need to add "whether talking concurrently or not."

34 There *should* be page numbers from page two onwards.

35 Method should *not* start on a new page.

36 The title "Method" should *not* be in bold or other different font type or size.

37 "Participants" should *not* be in bold, but *should* be in italics, and should *not* have a period after it.

38 It is not the *participants* who consist of males and females, but the *sample*!

39 Statistics letters like *M* and *SD* should be in italics.

40 You should state what the means are means of ($M = 25.0$ years, $SD = 9.1$).

41 You should also include other relevant demographics, in this case handedness, since the number in Results is less than the number in the sample.

42 Don't use abbreviations without first defining them.

43 Give an example of a scale item. In this case, say what sort of common tasks the EHI asks about.

44 For most scales, mention whether items need to be recoded, and that high scores mean more of that variable. In this case, say that a quotient was calculated to indicate degree of handedness.

45 The Method section should allow someone else to replicate your study. Give dimensions of dowels.

46 I know it's pedantic, but say that the task was to balance *the dowel* on the index finger!

47 You should also say what the verbal task was. In this study, there might be an effect on interference of the degree of difficulty of the verbal task, so it is important that a reader (or critic) knows exactly what you did.

48 There should be the heading *Procedure* here.

49 It is important that students were randomly assigned to pairs. Say so. Say that one was to be the instructor, and the other the participant.

50 Numbers less than 10 are spelt in full.

51 It is also important that the order of the trials was counterbalanced (to allow for learning effects). You need to say so.

52 Again, pedantic, but spell out that what was measured was how long the participant could keep the dowel balanced on their finger. It is another aspect of the study that could be a limitation - variation in what counts as "no longer balanced."

53 You should say that the instructions were in writing and read by the "instructor" in order to keep them uniform across participants.

54 Results should *not* start on a new page.

55 Results should not be in bold, but in ordinary 12-point font.

56 Table titles should have the first letter of major words in uppercase font.

57 There should *not* be a period after the title.

58 Tables should *never* have vertical lines in them, and horizontal ones should be kept to a minimum.

59 You should make clear that RS, RV etc, are the length of time in seconds.

60 Abbreviations like RS, RV etc, need a note at the end of the table, spelling out what they are. So does the fact that numbers in brackets are standard deviations. See the good example.

61 Do *not* repeat numbers that already exist in tables.

62 "Left hand times are not very different" from what? I know this can be deduced from the next sentence, but it should be unambiguous.

63 What hypothesis? The reader should not have to remember it. You can integrate it into a sentence by using "as expected" or "as predicted" when describing the results.

64 Again, what hypothesis. Spell it out again. It may seem repetitive, but in larger more complex lab reports, you will have two or more hypotheses, and will need to be specific.

65 You are only referring to right-handed males. Say so.

66 Index fingers, not "hands". Always be specific.

67 Do *not* repeat numbers from Results in the Discussion.

68 "females had almost the same time" as what? For balancing on either index finger while talking.

69 Prior research does not support new findings. New findings support (or otherwise) past findings. The present findings supported Kinsbourne and Cook (1971) and Johnson and Kozma (1977).

70 Again, "balanced longer" is too vague. Spell it out!

71 This is also ambiguous. "By hand" may mean comparing left with right hand (which was different), or comparing balancing while talking or not talking (which was not different).

72 Don't be too dogmatic. Say "Johnson and Kozma (1977) suggest that this is because…"

73 This explanation is actually quite good. It should have initially been in the Introduction

74 Too brief and conversational. Refer to balancing times.

75 This is also too vague. You should be less dogmatic, and say something like "It may be speculated that men are more used to such physical manipulations." If you can find a reference that backs this up that is even better.

76 This is too flippant for a formal lab report. See the section on "implications" on p. 72

77 Too vague. How could it apply?

78 Although for many studies, especially those looking at cognitive processes, students are unrepresentative of the general population, is there any reason to think that they would be different in this case? In fact, you could argue that students are more used to talking, and so they should have *less* interference!

79 That's a description, not a conclusion. What did you conclude from that observation?

80 "References" *does* start on a new page.

81 References in the reference list have the second and later lines indented.

82 The volume number should *also* be in italics.

83 What happened to Oldfield (1970). It is easy to omit a reference to a scale, but you need to reference everything you cite in the body of the report.

Appendix C
Answers to exercise

Independent and dependent variables

1	Independent:	Severity of initiation.
	Dependent:	Liking for the group.
2	Independent:	Size of the group.
	Dependent:	Whether subjects conformed or not.
3	Independent:	Distribution of practice.
	Dependent:	Time continuously on target.
4	Independent:	Type of association in the word pairs.
	Dependent:	How well the word pairs are recalled.
5	Independent:	Drug dose – real, placebo or none.
	Dependent:	Self-rating of nausea.
6	Independent:	Some measure of alcohol or cannabis intoxication (amount drunk or smoked?).
	Dependent:	Some measure of driving ability.
7	Independent:	Amount or type of childhood training in independence.
	Dependent:	Some measure of achievement motivation.
8	Independent:	Level of anxiety.
	Dependent:	Preference, either alone or with others.
9	Independent:	(i) Room temperature, and (ii) Presence or absence of distracting music.
	Dependent:	Accuracy of typing.
10	Independent:	Type of film sequence, either violent or non-violent.
	Dependent:	(i) Heart rate, and (ii) Blood pressure.

Appendix D
1000 commonly misspelled words

I have said earlier that markers don't usually take marks off for poor spelling. However, it does leave a bad impression. Since most word-processing programs have a spell-checker, poor spelling suggests that you haven't used it, and so have not given your document the thorough checking it deserves.

Markers are not usually concerned about words that are spelt differently by Americans and Australians (behavior and behaviour, respectively, or analyze and analyse). They are more concerned about whether you are being careless, because it suggests that you may have been careless in other areas too. Where a marker may have given you the benefit of the doubt about your understanding of the material if your expression is a little confusing here and there, she or he is less likely to do so if your spelling is poor, or if the document has obviously not been proofread.

In his very useful book on student skills, Burdess (1991) has a list of 1000 commonly misspelled words. He has kindly given me permission to reproduce the list here, so that you have no excuse for spelling any of them incorrectly, even if you don't have access to a word processor. Occasionally there are two versions of a word. Burdess suggests that these are words where no matter which variant is attempted, they are still often misspelled.

You may like to photocopy the list and pin it in some prominent place where you can consult it while you write.

a lot
abbreviate
abbreviation
abolition
absence
abundance
abundant
academic
academically
academy
accede
access
accessibility
accessible
accident
accidentally
acclaim
acclamation
accommodate
accommodation
achievable
achieve
achievement
achiever
achieving
acquaintance
acquiesce
acquire
acquit
acquitted
adamant
adapt
adaptation
address
adequate
adherence

adherent
adjective
administer
administration
administrative
advertisement
aerial
aggravate
aggravation
aggression
aggressive
aggressor
alcohol
alcoholic
alienate
alienation
align
alignment
allegation
allege
allegedly
allegiance
alleviate
allocate
allocation
allot
allotted
already
altogether
amend
amendment
among
amongst
amount
analogy
analyse, *or*
analyze (US)
analysis
analytical
analytically
ancillary
anecdotal
anecdote
annihilate
annoy
anonymity
anonymous
Antarctic
anxious
appal
appalled
appalling
apparatus
apparent
apparently
appeal
appealed
appealing
appear
appearance
appropriate
appropriately
archaeologist, *or*
archeologist
archaeology, *or*
archeology
Arctic
arguable
arguably
argue
argument
article
as well
ascertain
assistance
associate
association
assume
assuming
assumption
assurance
assured
assuring
asymmetrical
asymmetry
atrocious
atrociously
attach
attachment
attendance
attendant
authoritarian
authoritatively
authority
auxiliary
availability
available
avoid
awkward
awkwardly

bankruptcy
basically
beautiful
become
beggar
beginning
believable
believe
beneficial
benefit
benefited
benefiting
blatant
blatantly
boisterous
boundary
bourgeois
bourgeoisie
Britain
buoyant
bureau
bureaucracy
bureaucratic
business

calculable
calendar
campaign
cancel
cancellation
canister
capital
capitalism
capitalist
career
caricature
catalogue
catastrophe
catastrophic
categorise, *or*
categorize
category
ceiling
cemetery
censor
census
central
centralise, *or*
centralize
centrality
century
ceremonial
ceremony
challenge
changeable
character
chargeable
charisma
charismatic
chauvinism
chauvinist
chauvinistic
chief
choice
Christian
circuit
cognition

cognitive
coincide
coincidence
collaborate
collaborator
colleague
college
collegiate
collision
colonel
commemorate
commemoration
commend
commendable
commission
commit
commitment
committed
committee
commodity
comparative
comparatively
comparison
compatibility
compatible
compel
compelled
compensate
compensation
competent
competently
competitive
competitively
comprehend
comprehensible
comprehensive
computer
conceit
concept
conceivable
conceive
concentrate

concentric
concept
condemn
condemnation
condemned
connotation
conquer
conquered
conscience
conscientious
conscious
consciousness
consensus
considered
consistent
consolidate
constant
construe
construed
contemporary
contempt
contemptible
contradict
contradictory
contributor
control
controllable
controlled
controller
controversial
controversy
conurbation
convenience
convenient
corporal
correspondence
corroborate
corroboration
counterfeit
courteous
create
creation

criticise, *or*
criticize
criticism
cue
curriculum
cynic
cynicism

debatable
deceit
deceivable
deceive
decision
decrepit
deductible
defendant
defensible
defensive
definite
definitely
definition
degradation
delegate
delegation
deliberate
deliberately
demonstrate
demonstration
denigrate
denigration
deplete
depletion
description
desirable
despair
desperate
desperately
despite
deter
deteriorate
determine
deterred

deterrent
detriment
detrimental
devastate
develop
development
develops
deviance
deviancy
deviant
diaphragm
dichotomy
dietary
difference
different
dilapidate
dilapidation
dilemma
disappear
disappeared
disaster
disastrous
discernible
disciple
disciplinary
discipline
discretion
discriminate
discrimination
disintegrate
disintegration
dispensable
disprove
dissident
dissimilar
dissipate
distinct
division
doctor
dominance
dominant
dormant

dramatically
drunkenness
duly

earned
economically
ecstasy
eight
eighth
eliminate
elimination
embarrass
embarrassing
embarrassment
embryo
embryos
emigrate
emigration
eminent
eminently
emperor
emphasis
emphasise
encompass
encroach
encroaches
enforceable
enormous
environment
equilibrium
equip
equipment
equipped
equipping
erupt
eruption
essential
euthanasia
eventually
evolutionary
exaggerate
exaggeration
excel
excellence
excellent
excelling
excitable
excite
excitement
exemplify
exhilarate
exhilarating
exist
existence
existent
exorbitant
explain
explainable
explanation
explanatory
extraordinary

facilitate
facility
facsimile
familiar
fascinate
feasibility
feasible
February
feminine
femininity
feud
field
finally
finite
flamboyant
flexibility
flexible
fluorescent
forcible
forecast
foreign
foreigner
foresee
foreshadow
forest
forewarn
foreword
forfeit
fortunate
fortunately
fourteen
fourth (4th)
friend
further

gadgetry
galloped
gauge
ghettos
goddess
government
governor
graffiti
grammar
grief
grieve
guarantee
guaranteed
guard
guardian
guerilla
guidance

haphazard
harass
harassment
harmful
hazard
hazardous
helpful
helpfulness
hereditary
heterogeneous
hierarchical
hierarchy
hindrance
homogeneous
honorary
humorous
hygiene

identical
ideology
idiosyncrasy
immediate
immediately
immigrant
immigration
imminent
impenetrable
imperative
in fact
in turn
inadvertent
incidentally
incompatible
incurred
indefinite
indefinitely
independence
independent
indispensable
indistinct
indubitably
inevitable
infallible
infinite
infinitely
information
innate
innocuous
innuendoes
inoculate
insistence
insistent
insoluble

integrate
intensely
interest
interfere
interpret
interpreter
interpreting
interrupt
interruption
intervene
intricacy
investigator
involvement
irreconcilable
irreparable
irresistible
irreverent
irreversible
irrigation
irritation
Israel

jealous
jeopardise, *or*
jeopardize
jeopardy
journal
jubilant
jurisdiction

keenness
kilogram
knowledge
knowledgeable
known

laboratory
laid (not layed)
lawsuit
legitimacy
legitimate
leisure
leisurely
liaison
library
lieutenant
likeable
likelihood
literature
livable
livelihood
loneliness
lonely

machinery
maintain
maintenance
manageable
manoeuvre, *or*
maneuver (US)
marihuana, *or*
marijuana
mathematics
meant
Mediterranean
merely
message
messenger
meteorological
meteorology
microfiche
milieu
mimic
mimicked
mimicry
miniature
ministry
miracle
miscellaneous
mischievous
misconstrue
monitor
monotonous
monotony
motivate
motivation
murmuring
mystifying

naive
natural
naturally
necessarily
necessary
negative
negotiable
negotiate
nonsense
nostalgia
notable
notably
noticeable
nuclear
nuisance
nurture

obedience
obedient
objector
obsolescence
obsolescent
obsolete
obstacle
occasion
occasionally
occur
occurred
occurrence
occurring
offered
offering
official
officially
officious
omission
omit
omitted
opening
openness
opponent
opportunity
optimistic
ordinarily
ordinary
origin
original
outspokenness
override
overriding
overrule
overruling

paid (not payed)
palliative
paradigm
paraffin
parallel
paranoid
parliament
parliamentary
particular
particularly
patriarchal
patriarchy
peculiar
people
perceive
perceptible
performance
perhaps
permanent
permanently
permissible
perseverance
persistence
persistent
personnel
persuade

persuasive
pesticide
phenomena
phenomenon
Philippines
physical
physically
physician
piece
pinnacle
playwright
poison
poisonous
polar
policy
political
politician
pollution
positive
possess
possessive
practitioner
precede
precedence
precedent
precious
prefer
preference
preferred
preferring
prejudice
prejudicial
preparation
prepare
presence
prestigious
prevail
prevalence
prevalent
primary
privilege
privileged
procedure
proceed
process
procession
processor
profession
professional
proffer
proffered
proficiency
proficient
programmed
programming
proletariat
prominent
pronunciation
propeller
proponent
proprietor
proprietorial
prosperous
prove
psychiatric
psychiatrist
psychiatry
psychological
psychologist
psychology
publicly
punctuation
pursue

queried
query
querying
questionnaire
queue
queuing
quotient

racism
racist
really
recede
receive
recession
receipt
reciprocal
recommend
recommendation
reconcilable
refer
referee
reference
referral
referred
referring
refrigerator
regard
regarding
register
registered
registering
regrettable
regrettably
regular
regularly
reign
relative
relatively
relegate
relevance
relevant
religious
religiously
rely
reminiscence
reminiscent
repentant
repetition
repetitive
repetitively
research
researcher
resemblance
reservoir
resistant
resource
respectability
respondent
response
responsibility
restaurant
resuscitate
reticent
reveal
reversible
rhetorical
rhyme
rhythm
rigid
rigorous

sacrilege
sacrilegious
saleable
satellite
scenery
seaboard
secondary
secrecy
secretary
segregate
seize
sense
sensible
sensitive
separate
separately
sergeant
sheriff
sieve
signature
significance
significant
similar

similarly
sincere
sincerely
sizeable
sociable
solely
solicitor
souvenir
sovereignty
spacious
spaciousness
spatial
spatially
special
specially
spectacular
strategy
submit
subservience
subservient
substantial
substantially
subtle
subtly
success
successful
successfully
succinct
succinctly
suddenness
suffice
sufficient
suggest
summarise
summary
superb
superintendent
supersede
superseding
supplement
support
suppress
suppression
supremacy
survey
survive
survivor
susceptibility
susceptible
suspicious
suspiciously
sustain
sustenance
symmetrical
symmetrically
symmetry

taboo
taboos
taxied
taxiing, *or*
taxying
technical
technique
temperature
temporarily
temporary
tenant
tendency
tertiary
thorough
thought
threatened
through
throughout
tight
tobacco
tongue
totalitarian
transfer
transferable
transferred
transferring
transience
transient
triple
truly
twelfth
tyranny

unbelievable
underlie
undoubtedly
unfortunate
unfortunately
unmistakably
unnecessary
unparalleled
unrepentant
unsociable
until
up to
usage
useful
useless
utilise, *or*
utilize
vacuum
valuable
variable
variance
vegetable
vehicle
vengeance
versatile
vertical
vertically
vicious
viciously
view
vigorous
violence
violent
virtual
virtually
volcano
volcanoes
voluntarily
voluntary
vulnerable

warrant
Wednesday
whether
which
wholly
withdrawal
woollen
worshipper
worshipping
writing
written

yacht
yield

zeros

Glossary

acknowledgment *See* citation.

aims The aims of a study are the statements, in broad general terms, of the goals that you as the experimenter expect to achieve.

analytical categories These are the small and simple categories that you compare and contrast, or analyse in your essay. You develop them from larger ones in the question. For example, if a question asked you about the role of deception in social psychological research, you could break this down into the more manageable analytical categories of participants who don't know they are participants, minor deceptions like a misleading heading on a questionnaire, and more serious deceptions such as leading people to believe they are inflicting electric shocks on other people.

apparatus The instruments or equipment used in the running of an experiment (as distinct from paper and pencil tests, which are usually called 'materials').

argument An argument is a series of claims, some of which are called premises, and one of which is called the conclusion. The conclusion should follow logically from the premises.

assumptions These are beliefs or suppositions of the researcher, or even the whole society. Often they are not explicitly stated, or even things of which researchers are consciously aware. However, our assumptions tend to affect the questions we ask, our attitudes to people and research, and our behaviour. In the context of essays and lab reports, it is useful to try to become aware of the assumptions of the researcher you are reading.

bibliography A list of all the journal articles and books you consulted in the preparation of a report. You do *not* include a bibliography in a psychology lab report. *See also* reference.

citation A citation is the mentioning or acknowledgment in your text of the work of another person. If you write 'Smith and Jones (1989) suggest that . . .' you have made a citation of their work. Your reference list must include all the citations you have made in your report.

collaboration Collaboration means working together with other people in some joint activity. Check with your tutor or lecturer about the amount of collaboration acceptable when preparing for a lab report.

construct A construct is generally considered synonymous with the term 'concept'. In psychological terms, a construct is something that is not itself observable, but is assumed to exist because it can explain observable behaviour. An example is anxiety, which is not itself observable, but is assumed to be a mechanism that gives rise to emotions such as apprehension, distress, uneasiness and dread.

copying As distinct from collaboration, copying is definitely unacceptable. It means using the work of another student and passing it off as your own. Do not do this. *See also* plagiarism.

data Data are the body of facts gathered in an experiment or a study. The singular is 'datum'. 'Raw data' are data as they have been collected, before you have summarised them or analysed them in any way.

debriefing Debriefing is the explanation you give to a subject at the completion of a study or experiment. Such an explanation should include an overview of the theory the research relates to, the research question, your hypotheses and the relevance of what was done to the participant. If any deception was involved, the debriefing makes clear why it was necessary.

degrees of freedom These refer to the independent pieces of information known about a sample for which we are about to calculate a statistic. They are important because they give an idea about how powerful or informative the statistic is, and that is why they are reported when any statistical test is made.

dependent variable A dependent variable is a variable whose values are the result of changes in the values of other variables. In an experiment the dependent variable is what you actually measure. You are hoping that the values of it are 'dependent' on the other variables that you already know about (the 'independent variables').

descriptive statistics This phrase is a general label for procedures that organise and summarise collections of raw data. The most commonly used procedures are means and standard deviations. The procedures are descriptive because they simply describe the data; they do not draw any inferences about it.

design The design of an experiment refers to how the experiment was organised, that is, how many groups of subjects you had, and what procedures were carried out on each. In complex studies there is a separate subheading in the Methods section to explain the design.

empirical This term is used very loosely to cover a number of concepts. Most commonly it refers to the collection, analysis or evaluation of data. An empirical finding is something that has been actually observed, as distinct from something inferred or deduced. An empirical construct is one that has been inferred from observation of behaviour rather than deduced from a theory.

evidence In the context of psychology lab reports and essays, evidence is the data collected by researchers. The conclusions they have drawn from that data are a sort of evidence, as is any publication that is available to be checked, but such information is more questionable.

experiment An experiment is a set of conditions and procedures for testing a hypothesis. It emphasises control over independent variables, and the measurement of dependent variables so that cause-and-effect relationships can be determined.

extension In the context of lab reports, an extension is the allocation of more time to complete the assignment than was originally allowed. This situation will normally be permitted only in traumatic circumstances that can be documented in some way. Requests for extensions should be made to your tutor or lecturer before the original due date.

extraneous (nuisance) variable Sometimes called 'chance error', this term refers to the effects of variables that arise from chance, such as running the experiment on an uncomfortably hot day. Usually, with real-life experiments and large numbers of subjects, such errors tend to cancel each other out. In the context of student experiments, they may affect the outcome of the study, and you should be aware of their possible effect.

factor A factor is anything that has a causal influence on something else. It is often used interchangeably with 'independent variable', especially in writing about statistical procedures. Some of those procedures talk about 'levels' of a factor. This term refers to the magnitude of whatever the factor is, such as decibel level or dosage level.

generic Used in the sense of 'generic skills' it means more widely applicable than just to psychology.

hypothesis A hypothesis is any statement that could serve as an explanation of certain facts. It should be presented in such a form that it can be subjected to empirical test and then supported or not supported by the evidence.

independent variable This term refers to a variable where the values it can take are either manipulated, or controlled or recorded by an experimenter, so that their effect on some other variable (the dependent variable) can be observed. It is called 'independent' because, in principle, its values are not dependent on changes in the values of other variables.

inferential statistics Statistics of this kind are used when making inferences. They use the mathematics of probability theory to infer generalisations about populations from data taken from samples of those populations. The ones you will first come across are t-tests and analysis of variance.

manipulation (experimental) This term usually refers to controlling the values of an independent variable; for example, having three groups of subjects, each of which is given a different treatment.

measurement Measurement is the assigning of numbers to events or objects within strict rules. It might be as simple as obtaining people's height in centimetres, or as complicated as recording their intelligence according to IQ scores.

methodology Strictly speaking, methodology refers to the way in which knowledge and understanding are achieved. Many people use the term as synonymous with 'scientific method'. It is a much broader term than 'method', which refers to the particular procedures used in a specific investigation.

operationalisation Operationalisation refers to the procedure by which a theory gives rise to a specific hypothesis that is concrete and testable. For example, you might have a theory that says that attention is directly related to proximity of a stimulus. Such a statement is very broad. You could operationalise it to hypothesise that students at the front of the class would maintain more eye-contact with the lecturer than students at the back of the class. This statement is now a specific and testable hypothesis. If supported, it adds support to your theory.

organised scepticism This is the attitude that you won't believe what is said unless there is good evidence to back up the assertion. Organised scepticism is a fundamental property of good science – that it is the evidence that counts, not the authority of the scientist making the pronouncement.

participant A participant is a subject, someone who takes part in a study. You need to describe your participants, at least in general terms, so that your reader can decide how representative your results are for whatever group the reader is interested in.

placebo A treatment or preparation with no medicinal or pharmacological effects. It is used in studies of the effects of drugs to distinguish between real pharmacological effects and the psychological effects operating on subjects who believe they are being given the real drug.

plagiarism In simple terms plagiarism means 'copying'. It is used to refer to copying from someone else's published work without acknowledging the real source of the work. It is unacceptable because it is the academic equivalent of theft: taking the work of other people and using it as if it were yours. It does not simply apply to quoting the exact words of someone's published work without acknowledgment. Using someone's published ideas without acknowledgment is also plagiarism. You are encouraged to express other people's ideas in your own words, but you must make a reference in your report indicating that this is what you have done.

post hoc Latin for 'after this'. In the context of psychology it usually refers to statistical procedures used after an experiment has been run and some overall statistical significance found. These procedures determine which of several factors contribute to the overall significance.

primary source A primary source is a reference, such as a journal article or book, that you have actually read. *Contrast with* secondary source.

problem (research problem) A research problem is the question that you want to answer by running your study. In general terms, it is a situation where some of the components are known, and others need to be discovered.

proof, prove (evidence) Very loosely, proof is any demonstration that provides logical support for a belief. In the context of a lab report, I want to emphasise that you *cannot* prove anything! Your hypothesis can be supported, if the observed facts are in agreement with the propositions in your hypothesis, or it can fail to be supported if the observed facts are not in agreement with the hypothesis. Neither the hypothesis nor the theory from which it is derived can ever be proved.

qualitative Qualitative refers to differences in kind, so that apples are qualitatively different from oranges, or, more psychologically, some psychologists argue that the way children think is qualitatively different from the way adults think.

quantitative Something is quantitative if it is capable of being measured. To contrast quantitative with qualitative, your anxiety at being asked to recall the name of your 5th grade teacher is quantitatively different from your anxiety when sitting a psychology exam. The difference can be measured in some way.

questionnaire A questionnaire is any set of questions designed to be answered by a person, who is usually called a 'respondent' in this situation. Typically the questions will deal broadly with a single area of interest or a small number of such areas.

random sample A sample is a subset of a population. The students in your psychology class are a sample of the university population. However, they may not be representative of that population. A random sample is a sample taken so that every member of the population has an equal, independent probability of being selected.

reference In the context of a lab report, a reference is any material to which you refer in the body of the report. Typically, references will be journal articles or books, but in an essay they could also be newspaper articles, government reports, or television programs. *See also* primary source and secondary source.

replicate, replication To replicate an experiment is to reproduce exactly the method of the earlier experiment on a new sample of subjects. Because conclusions are drawn from experiments on the basis of probability, replication is important. Repeated similar findings add to the support for the hypotheses made, and by inference to the theories that produce the hypotheses. It is because replication is important to the scientific method that the Method section needs to be accurate enough for other experimenters to be able to reproduce your experiment exactly.

representative A 'representative sample' means that the characteristics of the sample are sufficiently like those of the population that you can make realistic judgments about the population on the basis of what you find about your sample.

sample A sample is a subset of a population. The students in your psychology class are a sample of the university population. However, they may not be representative of that population. *See also* random sample.

scale, subscale In the sense in which you will most frequently encounter it, a scale is a collection of questionnaire items that measure some psychological construct. An example would be an intelligence scale. A subscale is a subset of these items that measure some component of the overall variable, say the verbal ability subscale of an intelligence scale.

secondary source A secondary source is a reference that you have not read yourself, but has been referred to in something you did read. If you read in your textbook that Piaget (1932) came to some conclusion, but you do not have access to Piaget's actual article, then any statement you make about what Piaget said in that article must acknowledge where you read it, namely in your textbook, not in Piaget's original work.

significance level This is an arbitrary value, which you use as a criterion for deciding whether your observed data are different enough from what you could expect if only chance factors were operating, to consider your data to be statistically significant. It is frequently set at 5%. If p is the probability of the observed results or more extreme ones happening by chance alone, then '$p < .05$' shows that your data indicate a statistically significant result.

statistic A statistic is a number derived from some mathematical manipulation of your data, which summarises a characteristic of your sample, and theoretically reflects the population from which the sample was drawn. An example is the mean of your sample. The term 'statistic' is also applied to the number resulting from a statistical procedure. For example, the number you obtain when applying a t-test is a statistic.

study A psychological study is an investigation into some aspect of the thought or behaviour of people or, sometimes, other animals. It is often used as a more general term than 'experiment', because a study does not necessarily record or manipulate independent variables. A study may be an observation of behaviour, or a collection of information by questionnaire, or it may be an experiment.

survey A survey is a search for particular kinds of information. It generally refers to a study using questionnaires, interviews or established scales, for example, intelligence or aptitude scales.

theory A theory is a general principle advanced as an explanation for a set of known facts or empirical findings. Good theories can be used to deduce many hypotheses in different areas of application, which are then supported when tested empirically.

variable A variable is some characteristic of people or things that can change, either within the person, or between persons, things or situations. Variables can be as obvious as height or eye colour, or as complex as intelligence, ability to cope or marital satisfaction.

References

Albert, R.S. (1975). Toward a behavioral definition of genius. *American Psychologist, 30*, 140–151.

American Psychological Association. (2001). *Publication manual*. (5th ed.). Washington, DC: Author.

Betts, K., & Seitz, A. (1994). *Writing essays and research reports in the social sciences*. (2nd ed.). Melbourne: Thomas Nelson.

Braithwaite, V.A. (1987). The scale of emotional arousability: Bridging the gap between neuroticism construct and its measurement. *Psychological Medicine, 17*, 217–225.

Burdess, N. (1991). *The handbook of student skills for the social sciences and humanities*. Sydney: Prentice Hall.

Canobi, K.H., Reeve, R.A., & Pattison, P.E. (1998). The role of conceptual understanding in children's addition problem-solving. *Developmental Psychology, 34*, 882–891.

Cattell, R.B. (1965). *The scientific analysis of personality*. Baltimore: Penguin.

Christensen, H., Jorm, A.F., Mackinnon, A.J., Korton, A.E., Jacomb, P.A., Henderson, A.S., & Rodgers, B. (1999). Age differences in depression and anxiety symptoms: A structural equation modelling analysis of data from a general population sample. *Psychological Medicine, 29*, 325–339.

Collins, N.L., & Read, S.J. (1990). Adult attachment, working models, and relationship quality in dating couples. *Journal of Personality and Social Psychology, 58*, 644–663.

Connelly, L.S., Hasher, L., & Zacks, R.T. (1991). Age and reading: The impact of distraction. *Psychology and Aging, 6*, 533–541.

Cross, S., & Marcus, H. (1991). Possible selves across the lifespan. *Human Development, 34*, 230–255.

Dahlback, O. (1990). The social value of risk taking. *European Journal of Social Psychology, 20*, 531–535.

Edwards, A.L. (1957). *The social desirability variable in personality research*. New York: Dryden.

Fletcher, G.J.O., Simpson, J.A., Thomas, G., & Giles, L. (1999). Ideals in intimate relationships. *Journal of Personality and Social Psychology, 76*, 72–89.

Freeman, H.R. (1992). Effect of instructor gender and gender role on student willingness to take a psychology course. *Teaching of Psychology, 19*, 93–95.

Halford, W.K., Bouma, R., Kelly, A., & McD Young, R. (1999). Individual psychopathology and marital distress. *Behavior Modification, 23*, 179–216.

Kidder, L.H., & Judd, C.M. (1986). *Research methods in social relations*. (5th ed.). New York: Holt, Rinehart and Winston.

Kinsella, G., Ong, B., Murtagh, D., Prior, M., & Sawyer, M. (1999). The role of the family for behavioral outcome in children and adolescents following traumatic brain injury. *Journal of Consulting and Clinical Psychology, 67*, 116–123.

Lewin, K. (1948). *Resolving social conflicts*. New York: Harper & Row.

Macrae, K. (1989). *Psychology 1 course handbook*. Melbourne: Department of Psychology, La Trobe University.

Marshall, L.A., & Rowland, F. (1998). *A guide to learning independently*. (3rd ed.). Melbourne: Longman Cheshire.

Martyna, W. (1978). What does 'He' mean? *Journal of Communication, 28*, 131–138.

Maruff, P., Wilson, P.H., DeFazio, J., Ceritelli, B., Hedt, A., & Currie, J. (1999). Asymmetries between dominant and non-dominant hands in real and imagined motor task performances. *Neuropsychologia, 37*, 379–384.

McAuley, J.D., & Kidd, G.R. (1998). Effect of deviations from temporal expectations on tempo discrimination of isochronous tone sequences. *Journal of Experimental Psychology: Human Perception and Performance, 24*, 1786–1800.

McMahon, M., & Knowles, A. (1997). Psychologists' and psychiatrists' perceptions of the dangerous client. *Psychiatry, Psychology and the Law, 4*, 207–215.

Moore, B.N. (1995). *Making your case: Critical thinking and the argumentative essay*. Mountain View, California: Mayfield Publishing Company.

Murray, G., Rawlings, D., Allen, N.B., & Trinder, J. (2003). NEO Five-Factor Inventory scores: Psychometric properties in a community sample. *Measurement & Evaluation in Counseling Development, 36*, 131–140.

Neumann, D.L., Lipp, O.V., & Siddle, D.A.T. (1998). Dissociation between skin conductance orienting and secondary task reaction time: Time course with a visual discrimination task. *Australian Journal of Psychology, 50*, 35–42.

Pearson, K.L., & Love, A.W. (1999). Adolescents' value systems, preferred resolution strategies, and conflict with parents. *Australian Journal of Psychology, 51*, 63–70.

Pierce, G.R., Sarason, B.R., & Sarason, I.G. (1992). General and specific support expectations and stress as predictors of perceived supportiveness: An experimental study. *Journal of Personality and Social Psychology, 63*, 297–307.

Pope, K.S. (1980). *On love and loving*. San Francisco: Jossey-Bass.

Priestley, G., Roberts, S., & Piper, M-E. (1999). Returning to the scene: Reminders and context reinstatement enhance children's recall. *Developmental Psychology, 35*, 1006–1019.

Rastle, K., & Coltheart, M. (1999). Serial and strategic effects in reading aloud. *Journal of Experimental Psychology: Human Perception and Performance, 25*, 482–503.

Rohrmann, B. (1998). Assessing hazard information/communication programs. *Australian Psychologist, 33*, 105–112.

Rollings, S., King, N., Tonge, B., Heyne, D., & Young, D. (1998). Cognitive-behavioral intervention with a depressed adolescent experiencing school attendence difficulties. *Behavior Change, 15*, 87–97.

Sanders, M.R., Halford, W.K., & Behrens, B.C. (1999). Parental divorce and premarital couple communication. *Journal of Family Psychology, 13*, 60–74.

Schul, Y., & Burnstein, E. (1990). Judging the typicality of an instance: Should the category be accessed first? *Journal of Personality and Social Psychology, 58*, 964–974.

Simpson, J.A., Rholes, W.S., & Nelligan, J.S. (1992). Support seeking and support giving within couples in an anxiety-provoking situation: The role of attachment styles. *Journal of Personality and Social Psychology, 62*, 434–446.

Slaughter, V. (1998). Children's understanding of pictorial and mental representations. *Child Development, 69*, 321–332.

Smith, R.A. (1995). *Challenging your preconceptions: Thinking critically about psychology*. Pacific Grove, California: Brooks/Cole Publishing Company.

Sternberg, R.J. (1993). *The psychologist's companion: A guide to scientific writing for students and researchers*. (3rd ed.). New York: Cambridge University Press.

Townsend, M.A.R., Moore, D.W., Tuck, B.F., & Wilton, K.M. (1990). Headings within multiple-choice tests as facilitators of test performance. *British Journal of Educational Psychology, 60*, 153–160.

Index

APPLICATION FOR ADMISSION AS:

STUDENT SUBSCRIBER

Applicable 1 June 2003 to 31 May 2004					
Date of Application	Processing Fee (incl. GST)	GST	Pro-rata Base Subscription (incl. GST)	GST	TOTAL AMOUNT DUE
1/6 - 30/11	NIL	NIL	$92.50	$8.41	$92.50
1/12 - 31/5	NIL	NIL	$46.25	$4.20	$46.25

The Australian Psychological Society Ltd

ABN 23 000 543 788

A 'Tax Invoice'/Receipt will be issued following the processing of your application.

PERSONAL DETAILS

Dr ❑ Mr ❑ Mrs ❑ Ms ❑ Miss ❑ Other ❑ ______________

FAMILY NAME: ______________________________ (______________________________)

FORMER NAME, IF APPLICABLE

GIVEN NAMES: ______________________________ DATE OF BIRTH: ____________________

To ensure that we are always able to contact you and provide you with quality service, we ask that you supply two addresses. Your **Preferred Mailing Address** will be recorded as the address to which all correspondence will be sent. Your Alternate Address will be used to communicate with you should we have difficulty contacting you at your Preferred Mailing Address. In addition, your **Preferred Telephone Number** will be listed as your general contact telephone number for release upon request.

PREFERRED MAILING ADDRESS:

____

____

STATE: __________ POSTCODE: __________

PREFERRED TELEPHONE: (   )__________

PREFERRED FACSIMILE: (   )__________

ALTERNATE ADDRESS:

____

____

STATE: __________ POSTCODE: __________

ALTERNATE TELEPHONE: (   )__________

ALTERNATE FACSIMILE: (   )__________

PREFERRED E-MAIL:______________________________

ACADEMIC DETAILS

(a) DEGREES, DIPLOMAS and any further academic qualifications which have been **awarded**:

Name of Institution	Degrees / Diplomas / Other	Month & Year Completed

(b) COURSE(S) IN PSYCHOLOGY – Accredited Degree or Postgraduate studies **currently being undertaken** (e.g. BA /BSc /BPsych/Postgrad Dip Psych etc):

Name of Institution	Course names	Date of Completion

FOR OFFICE USE ONLY

Payment: Subscription $ __________ NOTES: ______________________________

____

Continued on page 2 ☛

CERTIFICATION

(To be completed by Psychology Co-ordinator, Psychology Lecturer or Head of Psychology Department of current course in which applicant is enrolled). Note: ALL applicants must ensure that this section is completed. Failure to do so will delay the processing of your application.

I hereby certify that the applicant, ________________________________, is enrolled in a subject which is part of a program accredited by the APS for membership purposes.

Signature: ______________________________ Date: ________________

Full Name (Please print clearly): ______________________________

Position / Title: ______________________________

Name of Institution: ______________________________

DECLARATION

I HEREBY DECLARE THAT:

1. All information submitted by me in this application is true to the best of my knowledge. I understand that any misleading statement, or omission, may be cause for rejection of this application.
2. If admitted as a Student Subscriber, I will be bound by the Society's Memorandum, Articles and By-laws and Code of Ethics and any other rules or regulations adopted by The Australian Psychological Society Limited. *(Copies of the above documents are available for inspection at the National Office of the Society.)*
3. I understand that, as outlined in By-law 21, I will no longer be eligible to be a Student Subscriber (a) one year after qualification for Associate Membership, or (b) upon ceasing to be enrolled in an accredited course.
4. I understand that my title, full name and general contact telephone may be released by the Society upon request.

Signature: ______________________________ Date: ________________

PRIVACY OF INFORMATION

1. We are committed to protecting your privacy, and the confidentiality and security of the personal information you provide.
2. The personal information provided by you on this form will be used to:
   - Assess your eligibility for membership
   - Provide members with access to and information about a range of current and future benefits
   - Identify your *Preferred Telephone Contact* number, which may be disclosed to the public and other members, and other details included within the Membership Directory (refer point 4 below for further details)
   - Provide the APS with statistics related to its membership.
3. If you do not provide us with this personal information, we may not be able to process your application.
4. The personal information you have provided on this form may be disclosed to persons and organisations as follows:
   a) organisations external to the APS that provide us with administrative assistance in the delivery of some of the services you receive.
   b) the APS may release your *Preferred Telephone Contact* number in response to a request from the public or another member. If you do not want this telephone number released, please write in confidence to the Director of Membership at the address shown above.
   c) If elected as a Member of the APS, your name, *Preferred Telephone Contact* number and the *Organisation* for which you work (as per page 2 of this application form) as well as the State in which you are located and your membership of APS Colleges and Divisions will appear (unless otherwise directed by you) in the Directory of Members available on the APS Website. **Your other details, including address information, will remain confidential.** If you do not wish to be included in the Directory of Members, or you wish to be included but do not want your *Preferred Telephone Contact* number and/or the *Organisation* for which you work listed, please write in confidence to the Director of Membership at the address shown on the last page of this form.
5. You have the right to access personal information held by the APS that relates to you, subject to the exceptions in the Privacy Act 1988, and to correct such information which is not accurate. Please contact the APS National Office with any such request.
6. For more information on the Society's policies regarding privacy, refer to the APS Website at www.psychsociety.com.au. Copies of the full APS Privacy Policy may be obtained from the APS National Office on request.

PAYMENT

1.If you are paying by **cheque**, please make payable to: The Australian Psychological Society Ltd. (Australian Dollars only please).

2.If you are paying by **credit card,** please complete the following details:

APS VISA ☐ Bankcard ☐ Mastercard ☐ VISA ☐ Amount: $ ____________

Card Number: ☐☐☐☐ ☐☐☐☐ ☐☐☐☐ ☐☐☐☐ Expiry Date: ____________

Card Holder's Name *(please print)*: ______________________________

Card Holder's Signature: ______________________________ Date: ____/____/____

RETURN FORM TO

Once you have completed this form, please return it together with **TOTAL AMOUNT DUE** (refer page 1) to:

Directorate of Membership
The Australian Psychological Society Ltd
PO Box 38 Flinders Lane PO
MELBOURNE VIC 8009
AUSTRALIA

Telephone enquiries to the Directorate of Membership on 03 8662 3300 or 1800 333 497 (toll free).

Email enquiries on *membership@psychsociety.com.au*

5/2002